RECUERDOS

A collection of true stories, give or take a little embellishment here and there, of the U.S. Border Patrol as told by present-day and retired Border Patrol officers, collected and edited by Gene Botts.

Board of Trustees
United States Border Patrol Museum and Memorial Library Foundation
4315 Trans Mountain Road
El Paso, Texas 79924
Telephone: (915) 759-6060

Contents

Foreword

I approach the writing of this *foreword* with great pride and humility. Being a Border Patrol officer is a unique experience shared by relatively few people. The sense of *camaraderie* and the *esprit de corps* of Border Patrol officers, both active and retired, is unparalleled.

Our Border Patrol traditions started with the first mounted U.S. Customs inspectors designated *Chinese Exclusion Officers* in 1893 and sent out to patrol the Mexican border in Texas, New Mexico, Arizona, and California to prevent the illegal entry of Chinese aliens into the United States. Then in 1903 the Immigration Service, then in the Department of Commerce, established a very few positions called *Mounted Border Guards*, whose duty it was "to keep out Chinese, thieves, and other undesirables and to guard against all forms of lawlessness on the border." The Mounted Border Guards were re-designated *Mounted Immigrant Inspectors* in 1917, but their duties remained substantially the same until 1920 when enforcing *prohibition* laws was added to their responsibilities.

The United States Border Patrol, as we know it, was established as an enforcement arm of the

Immigration Service in the Department of Labor on May 24, 1924. The original authorized force was 450 officers whose principle duty was to patrol the land borders and prevent the illegal entry of aliens into the United States. The Mounted Immigrant Inspectors became the nucleus of the new force and the ranks were filled-out by former Texas Rangers, former sheriff's deputies and police officers, and men who had applied for jobs as railroad mail clerks.

The Immigration Service was transferred to the Department of Justice in 1940, and then in 1943 the Bureau of Immigration and the Bureau of Naturalization were combined into the Immigration and Naturalization Service. For the next sixty years the Border Patrol was a branch of the INS. With the government reorganization and the birth of the Department of Homeland Security in the spring of 2003, the Border Patrol became a part of U.S. Customs and Border Protection.

The duties and authorities of today's Border Patrol Agents in many ways remain the same as in previous years, but they have been broadened to include narcotics enforcement and anti-terrorist activities. Technical equipment routinely used today is beyond anything that we could have imagined in my day.

When I was appointed to the Border Patrol on February 7, 1941, we had an on-duty force of about a thousand officers to cover both the border with Mexico and our border with Canada. My starting salary was $1,800 per annum.

Today the authorized force of the Border Patrol is more than 12,000 officers, and the starting salary is a minimum of $34,005 per annum, and some trainees, depending upon their individual qualifications, start at even higher salaries. The average journeyman Border

Patrol Agent after three years service today earns more than $62.500 a year.

My, how times have changed! But the one thing that has not changed from one generation to the next over all of the years is the loyalty, dedication to duty, and *esprit de corps* constantly and continually displayed by all Border Patrol officers and employees.

All of the men and women who took the time to record these interesting stories of Border Patrol days are to be commended. This is an important part of the rich history of the Border Patrol to be enjoyed by all of us and future generations, as well. This effort is especially commendable as all of the proceeds from the sale of this book will go toward financing the future operations of the Border Patrol Museum. How our museum evolved from an idea into the beautiful, modern institution that it is today is another interesting story.

In the fall of 1978, thirty-four recently retired former Border Patrol officers met in Denver, Colorado, for the purpose of establishing a fraternal organization comprised of former colleagues. After several meetings and considerable discussion, the **Fraternal Order of Retired Border Patrol Officers** (FORBPO) was born. Officers were elected, and it was decided that we would meet annually at different locations about the country to socialize and renew old friendships.

Our first annual meeting was held in Tucson, Arizona, in the spring of 1979. During that meeting, someone suggested that in addition to being merely a social organization we should sponsor some worthwhile project to promote the United States Border Patrol and its history, such as a museum.

The membership was polled, and by a vote of three hundred twenty who were in favor to eleven who were opposed, the establishment of a Border Patrol Museum under the sponsorship and direction of the Fraternal Order of Retired Border Patrol Officers was authorized. Members of a Board of Trustees were selected, bylaws written and adopted, and in 1980 the National Border Patrol Museum and Memorial Library Foundation was incorporated in the State of Texas as a nonprofit organization. Subsequently, tax exempt status was received from the United States Internal Revenue Service.

Raising funds to get started was a challenge, but with a series of grants, donations, and the proceeds of our annual raffles, we were able to open our museum in 1985 in the basement of the Cortez Building in downtown El Paso, Texas. It was soon evident that the space was too small, but we had no other at the time.

After five years, our lease on the space in the Cortez Building expired, and we had to move. The Board of Trustees decided that we would not reopen until we had our own building. All of the artifacts were packed and placed in storage.

After hearing our plans, the El Paso City Council gave us a long term lease on approximately two acres of land on Transmountain Highway, north of the city and very near to where the Border Patrol Academy had once been located, for a dollar a year. All we had to do was come up with the money to build a suitable building.

Through another series of grants and donations, raffles and schemes such as selling bricks in the new building with the donors' names engraved on them, and a very generous donation of $150,000 by the Anthony L. Oneto American Legion Post in Los Angeles, California, which is comprised exclusively of INS officers, past and present, we raised the money.

The museum was reopened in February of 1994 in our beautiful 10,200 square foot building with an impressive dedication ceremony attended by several hundred dignitaries and officers and former officers and their families from all over the country.

Our museum continues to grow, getting bigger and better every year, thanks to the hundreds of volunteers and supporters who are building a legacy to be appreciated and enjoyed by generations to come.

Donald R. Coppock

Chief of the United States Border Patrol (Ret.)

Former Chairman of the Board of Trustees, National Border Patrol Museum and Memorial Library Foundation (20 years).

I Am A Citizen!

by

Ed Woods

In the year of sixteen fifty four
Relatives of mine came ashore
Relief of oppression they came
Revered these shores with my name

Revolutionary War I can brag
A relative built the first flag
All came here of one mind
Made the best of land they find

A new chance to live a way
Free from oppressions of the day
Cast their will upon a writ
Constitution, Bill of Rights, a candle lit

Rule of law which we now abide
Oath of allegiance in order to reside
One stick you may easily break
Bunched together, no man can take

Our laws not made for aliens to wander
Nor politicians to sidetrack and squander
The law constituted equal for all

Recuerdos

Live the law or you must fall

Thru all the wars my Grandfathers fought
My Father and I went without a thought
My Brother in Vietnam did serve
We followed the course, did not swerve

Now all those aliens violating our shore
Smuggling of people, drugs, and more
I cannot abide breakers of our laws
It is time to fight foreigners with flaws

Weak politicians looking for votes
Selling out my Country for a note
A dollar here, a dollar there
They strip our country bare

Tradition calls for action now
Arise American Citizens, I allow
Protest and guard our country
Bring back honor and sovereignty

December 2003

\+ + + + + + +

Jeff Milton
by

Gene Botts

So long as free people burnish the bright badge of courage, cherish the traditions of genuine chivalry, and revere the memory of honorable men, so long they should not forget him.

J. Evetts Haley

Jeff Milton is a legend, and as it is with most legends, especially those of the American Southwest in the 19th Century, it's often difficult to separate the facts from the wild stories made up by pseudo local historians and western writers over the years. I'm going to stick to the facts as I believe them to be. I'm convinced from what I have read of the man and what I have been told by people who knew him that he would be upset to read something about himself that wasn't true, even if it were flattering.

Jeff Milton wasn't the *first* border patrolman, as has been alleged by some writers, but he was among the first of the mounted inspectors who patrolled our border and enforced our immigration laws in the early years. He was tough, sometimes stubborn, and often difficult to deal with, but he was also a gentleman of the old school who put personal honor and integrity at the top of any list of virtues. He was an outstanding lawman in his time, and his story needs no embellishment.

Jefferson Davis Milton came into the world at the family cotton plantation about six miles from Marianna, Florida, on November 7, 1861. He was the tenth and last child of John Milton, who was then Governor of the Confederate State of Florida, and his second wife, Caroline (Howze) Milton.

Jeff was born into a family of affluence and prominence. His great-grandfather, John Milton, had served as an officer in the Revolutionary War and later as Georgia's State Secretary, and his grandfather, Colonel Homer Milton, fought in the War of 1812 and in the Seminole War. His father had been a successful lawyer in Georgia before he moved to Florida where he continued practicing law and established a cotton plantation, which he named *Sylvania*.

Shortly before Jeff's birth, the rumblings of discontent in the Southern States, which would ultimately lead to the Civil War, caused his father to enter politics, and in 1860 he was elected governor of the state.

Sylvania was a large and profitable plantation, which supported the Milton family, a few white *employees*, and some fifty negro slaves. The Milton family lived a life of relative luxury and privilege for the times, but harder times were just ahead.

Jeff's father had been one of the strongest supporters of the Confederacy, and the Union triumph in 1865 completely devastated him. He fell into a state of inconsolable depression, and the following year he ended his own life.

Jeff's mother, Caroline Milton, surprised everyone by taking up the reins of plantation management after her husband's suicide. Most of the few white employees and the majority of the former slaves continued working on the plantation under her direction after the war, but the turbulent political, economic, and social conditions of the time made her job exceedingly difficult. The plantation was never again as profitable as it had been, and the luxuries and privileges of the Milton family dwindled. The children's relationship with their mother also suffered; she no longer had the time or the energy to tolerate the normal squabbles and mischief of her offspring, and she became a stern master.

There is ample reason to believe that young Jeff may have been somewhat rebellious as a teenager. When he was sixteen years old, he left home and traveled alone to Navasota, Texas, a small frontier settlement about a hundred fifty miles northwest of Houston.

Jeff's older sister had married the year before and moved to Navasota with her husband who owned a general store there. Young Jeff worked in the store as a clerk for a while, but the confinement and the daily routine didn't suit him. He yearned for a more active life of adventure in the outdoors, and he decided to move on westward. He had some vague idea of becoming a cowboy or a Buffalo hunter.

He bought a horse and a saddle and a few other things that he thought he would need on the trail, and he set out for Fort Griffin, which was about thirty miles northeast of Abilene and reputed to be the center of Buffalo hunting in Texas at the time. Although he wasn't yet seventeen years old, traveling alone through the primitive and dangerous country didn't seem to bother him in the least.

A few weeks later, Jeff turned up in Fort Griffin, but Buffalo hunting turned out to be much different than he had imagined. He would have had to start at the bottom of the trade, which would have had him skinning and butchering in the open range amid millions of flies and an overwhelming stench. He wanted no part of it, and he soon found a job more to his liking on a nearby cattle ranch. The work was, of course, hard and dirty, and the pay was little, but he liked it, at least in the beginning.

In the fall he was sent out alone to winter pasture a herd of horses. He spent almost four months that winter with no human contact except for a few Indians who seemed to be constantly creeping around his camp trying to steal his horses. He had been given a few supplies, but for the most part he had to live off the land. His only shelter from the weather was a canvas tent that had more leaks than he could patch. By the time spring came around, he was beginning to seriously question the cowboy life, but he stayed on for several months during that summer. Fall of that year, however, found him back in Navasota working in his brother-in-law's general store.

Shortly after returning to Navasota, Jeff became acquainted with two young men about his own age who were also bored with their less than exciting lives and dreaming of adventure. One of them mentioned the Texas Rangers during one of their conversations, and the three of them started talking about the possibility of joining the Rangers. Jeff talked it over with his brother-in-law, and to his surprise his brother-in-law encouraged him.

In the early summer of 1880, armed with a letter of recommendation signed by his brother-in-law and another signed by a prominent lawyer in Navasota, Jeff Milton and his two friends set out on horseback for Austin to join the Texas Rangers. Not one of them had ever met a Texas Ranger, and they had no idea of what they were getting into.

Jeff was eighteen years old at the time. It's been said that he lied about his age in order to be accepted by the Rangers, as anyone less than twenty-one years of age was not eligible. I have serious doubts about that story; I don't think that it would have been necessary for him to lie.

Today the Texas Rangers are a modern and effective state law enforcement organization, well-trained and very selective in their recruiting. They like to give the impression that they were always so, but it's not true. In the summer of 1880 Texas Ranger was not a great job. Living conditions and working conditions for Rangers were harsh to say the very least, and it was damn dangerous work. There has never been a complete and accurate count of the number of Texas Rangers who gave their lives in service to Texas in the 19th Century, but the Texas plains are scattered with Ranger graves, some marked and some not. Texas asked quite a lot of the Rangers, but the state government didn't offer a lot in return. The pay was meager, and Rangers were expected to provide their own horse, saddle, weapons, clothes, and traveling kit. About the only thing that the state furnished in the way of equipment was a tent and ammunition. And the latter was to be used for *business* only; if a Ranger wanted to practice with his weapons, he had to buy extra ammunition with his own money. Some food was provided on the trail and in Ranger encampments, but it had to be constantly supplemented with game that the Rangers hunted and butchered for themselves. And a Ranger seriously wounded or crippled in the line of duty to the extent that he could not continue in the service was simply discharged to fend for himself. It was a tough way of life, and there weren't a lot of men standing in line to become Texas Rangers.

When Jeff Milton and his companions arrived in Austin in July of 1880, the Texas Rangers may have had a long list of qualifications for enlistment, perhaps including that the applicant be twenty-one years of age, but the prerequisites were mostly ignored. The only qualifications that mattered were that the applicant have two arms and two legs, appear to be reasonably healthy, be able to ride a horse, and be able to handle his weapons without shooting himself or his companions.

Jeff was sworn in the day that he arrived; he probably wasn't even asked about his age. And when he arrived at the Ranger encampment he was probably greeted by men many of whom were not much older than he, some may have been even younger. They were exactly what the Texas Rangers wanted and needed at that time: youngsters full of piss and vinegar and confident that they were invincible.

After a brief indoctrination and training period, no more than a couple of weeks, Jeff was sent to join Company 'B' encamped at Hackberry Springs.

Company 'B', as were most Ranger companies of that era, was comprised of a mixture of former Confederate soldiers who had never gotten over the sound of the bugle and the rush of battle, a few misfits trying to find their way in a changing world that was quickly passing them by, and young men, many in their teens, feeling their oats and looking for action and adventure. Young Jeff Milton fit right in with them as they set about enforcing the law and keeping the peace, such as was possible, in the riotous frontier towns, railroad construction camps, and cattle ranges of Southwest Texas.

Many stories have been told of Jeff's exploits during this period of his life. Those stories that he told himself in later years are probably true, or mostly true, and the rest were made up by the pseudo historians and writers over the years. I'll not try to sort them out; it's enough to say that it was hard and dangerous work, but Jefferson Davis Milton proved himself up to it in every way.

The usual enlistment in the Texas Rangers was for one year, but many, especially the younger men, enjoyed the challenge and the excitement of *rangerin'*, and they stayed longer. Jeff stayed with the Rangers almost three years; he took his discharge at Fort Davis in May of 1883. He never explained exactly why he left the Rangers when he did, but it was probably because he just got tired of it. It was a hard life and not very rewarding in terms of dollars and cents, and that's why most of them left when they did.

After he left the Rangers, Jeff took a job as a clerk in a dry goods store in Fort Davis. He was sleeping in a bed every night, eating better, and he had a little money in his pocket for a change, but boredom and restlessness soon set in again. He simply wasn't cut-out to be a storekeeper, and he began looking for something else.

He went into a partnership with another man in a saloon, but that didn't work out either. He clearly didn't have the patience necessary to succeed as a bartender, and he sold his half interest in the saloon and went into the freighting business with a friend using rented mules. "We was makin' Rangers' wages without the food and none of the fun," he later told a friend. After the first trip, they dissolved the partnership, and Jeff went back to his job in the dry goods store. He still didn't like the confinement and the boredom, but he was earning a fair living. Then in the fall of the year, an old friend came to his rescue. "Charlie Nevill quit the Rangers an' got himself elected sheriff. He wanted me to be his deputy in Murphyville, an' I didn't hold back."

He had no more than arrived in Murphyville when the railroad agent sought him out and told him that there was a gang of rowdy cowboys drunk and raising hell in the saloon. They were threatening to run the new deputy sheriff out of town as soon as he arrived. Jeff unpacked his double barrel ten-gauge shotgun and calmly walked to the saloon.

The cowboys, about a dozen of them, were bellied-up to the bar with their backs to the door, and Jeff was behind them cocking both barrels of the shotgun before they realized that he was there. As Jeff later told the story to J. Evetts Haley: "Boys, every one of you get them six-shooters off as fast as you can or I'll kill every damn one of you right here! Believe me, they shucked 'em. Then I made quite a talk to them, like a man would talk to men. I told them that they all wanted to be gentlemen when they came to town, to pull their six-shooters off and leave them behind the bar, and it had quite an effect on them. Never had no more trouble, not a word. After that they heaped their Colts on the counter with pleasure." The tension was broken, and one of the smiling cowboys bought him a drink. From his years with the Texas Rangers, he had learned well how to handle an unruly crowd from behind a shotgun.

In later years when Jeff would tell the story of his first day in Murphyville, he would say," I knew it was all whiskey talk. They was all good boys just celebrating a little bit an' out to have some fun. They wasn't gonna shoot nobody, and I didn't intend to shoot nobody, either. O'course, if one of 'em had started somethin', I'd have had to kill him. Wouldn't have been anything else I could do."

Murphyville was a new settlement in Jeff Milton's time there, and it was as wild and rough as any other frontier town, but unlike many of the others that sprang up along the railroad, it would grow and prosper in the years to come. In 1888 the name was changed to Alpine, Texas, the name that it bears today.

Jeff liked Murphyville, and he liked his job. He probably intended to stay indefinitely, but it wasn't to last. He was bunking in with the railroad freight agent in the railroad station when he fell ill in the fall of 1883. The local doctor diagnosed pneumonia, which in 1883 was as close to a death sentence as a man could come. Pneumonia was considered to be incurable and fatal in all cases. The railroad agent agreed to watch over him and care for him until he died, but Jeff didn't die. Either the doctor misdiagnosed his illness or pneumonia was *not* fatal in all cases. He was seriously ill for several weeks, but he eventually made a full recovery. Unfortunately, by the time that he got back on his feet, he had been replaced and another man was deputy sheriff in Murphyville.

Although the date isn't certain, it was probably in March of 1884 when he packed his few belongings, saddled his horse, and rode to El Paso. He didn't stay long in El Paso; a few days at most, and then he went on into New Mexico. He later told friends that he was headed for Socorro, which was booming at the time, but he ran out of money. When he arrived in San Marcial he was down to a lucky gold piece that he didn't want to spend and a few pennies. He quickly found work as a cowboy on the Illinois Cattle Company ranch. The ICC ranch was a large corporation cattle ranch that stretched for miles in every direction, and they were almost always in need of hands. Over the next few years, he would work on the ICC ranch on several occasions, but never for very long at a time.

Jeff's tracks are hard to follow at this time in his life. His independent nature and his insistence upon doing things *his way*, which was often different from the way his boss wanted something done, seems to have brought him into conflict with a number of bosses, and he would get fired or quit in the heat of an argument and move on to something else. He had a number of jobs, and he often had more than one job at the same time, which tends to confuse the record.

Charles Russell, a former Texas lawman, not the noted western artist and sculptor of that name, was elected sheriff in Socorro County, New Mexico, in 1885. Owing largely to Jeff's reputation and service in the Texas Rangers, Russell took him on as a deputy. It was probably a part-time job, as Jeff was also working on the ICC ranch and trying to do improvement work on a homestead of his own at this time. He was also a part-time range detective for the Central New Mexico Stock Growers Association. Jeff was apparently, wearing several different hats at the same time. Nevertheless, he is credited with bringing a large number of outlaws to justice, or to what passed for justice in New Mexico at the time. They were mostly cattle rustlers, but there was also a mixed bag of thieves and murderers among them.

It was during this time that the often told story of how Jeff Milton single-handedly saved twelve rustlers from a mass lynching occurred. There is more than one version of the tale, but the most probable version is the way Jeff told it himself: He was wearing his deputy sheriff and range detective hats concurrently, and he was leading a posse of about a dozen volunteers rounding up known cattle rustlers. They had twelve men in custody and were on their way back to Socorro to turn them over to the court for trial. The trail was hard and the weather was lousy, and one of the posse members suggested that they just hang the rustlers then and there and be done with it. Several of the others seem to concur. Jeff stood up, jacked a round into his rifle, and said, "Nothin' doin' boys. I'm not in that kind of business." One by one, the others soon came to their senses and realized that hanging their prisoners would be murder, and that was the end of it. Stories like this, especially if they took place in the Old West, tend to grow and get better with age. Years later, Jeff told his biographer, J. Evetts Haley, "These wa'n't bad men; they was just cow thieves."

Jeff Milton filed on two homesteads while he was in New Mexico, and he twice started to build a ranch for himself. He didn't finish either project. After he made the necessary improvements to gain title to the land on the first homestead, he sold it to the Illinois Cattle Company and used the money to visit his family in Florida. His title to the second homestead was challenged, and he lost the land in an adverse court decision. He always thereafter claimed that he was cheated by a crooked federal land agent and a corrupt judicial system, but the facts do not necessarily support him. It's more likely that he was the victim of his own lack of knowledge of the law and his lack of skill in land surveying and map reading. He seems to have filed a homestead claim on one parcel of land and then set about making improvements to another parcel. Before he finished making the necessary improvements to gain title to the land, someone else came along and homesteaded it.

After he lost the second homestead, Jeff was soured on New Mexico. He turned in his deputy sheriff badge, quit his job as a range detective, and set out for the Arizona Territory.

Commodore Perry Owens had recently been installed as sheriff of Apache County, in the Arizona Territory. Jeff, who had earned a reputation in Socorro County, New Mexico, that preceded him into Arizona, was made a deputy sheriff almost as soon as he arrived. He didn't hold the job long, though. He had a personality clash with Sheriff Owens, and he resigned in a huff after only a week. "I just didn't like the man," he would later tell friends.

It's not surprising that they didn't get along. Commodore Perry Owens was a *shoot first and ask questions later* kind of lawman. Commodore was his first name, not a military rank; he was named at birth for the famous naval officer and diplomat who opened Japan to trade from the West. He had no experience as a lawman before he became Apache County Sheriff, and he was probably afraid of most of the men that he was called upon to arrest. He always made sure that he had the *edge* before he made his move, and he left a bloody trail behind him in Apache County. He served only one term as sheriff and then a short period of time as a Deputy U.S. Marshal before he got out of law enforcement and became a storekeeper. He and Jeff Milton would have had little in common.

Having nowhere else in particular to go and being again unemployed, Jeff returned to El Paso where an old friend interceded with the Collector of Customs to help him get a job as a Mounted Customs Inspector. The El Paso Customs district at the time extended from Presidio, Texas, westward to the Colorado River. Jeff was appointed on March 11, 1887, and assigned to the Tucson office to patrol the Arizona border enforcing customs laws.

When Jeff Milton started with the Bureau of Customs in 1887 there were no designated immigration enforcement officers anywhere in the United States. Although the Chinese Exclusion Law was enacted in 1882, there were no provisions made for a separate force of officers to enforce the law. Customs inspectors, presumably including the mounted inspectors, enforced the few immigration laws then on the books along with their other duties. It wasn't until 1893 when selected inspectors were designated Chinese Exclusion Officers and sent out to patrol the border. Such designation in the Bureau of Customs was considered a promotion, which included a raise in salary for the inspectors selected.

When Jeff reported to the Deputy Collector of Customs in Tucson, he was told that his headquarters would be the Tucson office, but he would be responsible for the border with Mexico from Nogales, Arizona, to the Colorado River, three hundred miles of the roughest, most desolate desert terrain in the United States. He would be paid a flat salary of one hundred dollars a month, and he would be expected to furnish his own horse, whatever equipment he might need, and food. That was part of the bargain, and he would not be reimbursed or paid any subsistence allowance. Actually, considering the average pay of a law enforcement officer at the time, it wasn't a bad deal.

Jeff moved down to the border alone to begin his patrolling. He established his base camp in Aravaca, Sonora, Mexico, and he did much of his border patrolling from the south side of the line. He thought nothing of it, and his superiors in Tucson either didn't know about it or didn't care. There is some reason to believe that some of his arrests were made on the south side of the line in Mexico, as well, but that didn't seem to bother anyone, either.

When Jeff caught smugglers, as he did on many occasions, he would have to take them to Tucson for prosecution, a three or four day trip depending on where on the border he caught them. All of this, of course, he accomplished on horseback. He didn't complain, though; he thought that he was lucky to have such a great job.

After a few months of working alone, Jeff was sent a partner, Ben Hamilton. They rented an adobe house together on the Aguirre ranch, near Sasabe, and thereafter they did their patrolling from there. Living together and working together was probably a little too much togetherness. It wasn't long until they had a personality clash, and from then on each man did his patrolling alone. They didn't see much of each other except in passing, and they hardly spoke.

The following spring, Jeff discovered that there was a vacancy for a mounted inspector in the San Pedro River Valley. He was sick of working with Ben Hamilton, who was apparently more of a political hack than a lawman, and he applied for transfer.

In May of 1888, he was transferred to the Tombstone Customs office to patrol the border in the San Pedro River Valley. All of the inspectors working there were former Texas Rangers, and Jeff fit in immediately. He was partnered with *Captain* C.B. Kelton, a fellow southerner who shared his disposition and much of his outlook on life.

Kelton was just another mounted inspector. He was too young to have served in the Civil War, and he had not been a Captain in the Texas Rangers. No one seemed to know where he had acquired the title, but everyone called him *Cap* or *Captain*, just the same. He and Jeff were assigned to work a stretch of the border from the New Mexico line to Nogales. They got along and worked well together.

Tombstone at the time seemed to be a magnet for former Texas Rangers, as well as for Texans and other Southerners in general. They were all over the place, and several of them had important positions in the community. The role of the Texas Rangers in the evolution of the American Southwest outside of Texas has never been adequately recognized in history books or even in Western fiction. In the California goldfields of 1850 and the cattle camps and mining towns of New Mexico, Colorado, Arizona, and California well into the early years of the 20th Century, former Texas Rangers spread out and brought order to chaos wherever they went. They often assumed leadership roles on the frontier, and their contribution to the development of the West was way out of proportion to their numbers.

Jeff Milton thought that his life was pretty good in Tombstone, but all good things eventually come to an end. President Benjamin Harrison, a Republican, replaced President Grover Cleveland, a Democrat, in the White House in 1889. The Collectors of Customs and all of the officers, even the mounted inspectors, occupied political patronage jobs at that time, and when a new administration came to power, especially a new administration of the rival political party, they all lost their jobs. It was a hell of a way to run a government, but that's the way it was in 1889. They all knew that it could happen to them, of course. They expected that it would happen eventually, but they weren't expecting it in 1889. President Cleveland was popular, and they had all expected him to be re-elected. He would, in fact, be elected to a second term, but not until 1892.

Jeff was reluctant to leave, but he had to earn a living, and there wasn't much in the way of job prospects that appealed to him in Tombstone. Production at the mines was dropping off and the local economy was beginning to suffer. Most of his former Texas Ranger friends who had also lost their jobs moved on to other places looking for work. He and a friend passed the time hunting and prospecting, but they weren't making enough money at either to survive. He soon had to move to Tucson in search of employment.

Shortly after Jeff arrived in Tucson, he got sick with Smallpox, and he spent almost a month recovering in quarantine. When he recovered enough to ride a horse, he and a friend took an extended hunting and prospecting trip through the Papago Reservation, which is now called the Tono O'odam Reservation, and into Mexico. White men hunting on the Indian reservation didn't apparently bother anyone in those days, nor did wandering in and out of Mexico without official sanction on hunting and prospecting trips. Mexicans freely wandered back and forth across the line, as well, and so long as they weren't smuggling anything, no one bothered them.

The hunting was fun, and they bagged a lot of game, but they wound up giving most of the meat to the Indians. In his lifetime, Jeff Milton may have furnished more meat to Arizona Indians than the government Indian agents. The prospecting was another matter. They dug holes and busted rocks for days on end, but they didn't recover an ounce of metal of any kind. It was wasted time and labor, and they went back to Tucson broke and disgusted.

Unable to find a decent job that suited his particular talents, tastes, and temperament, Jeff began trading in horses and mules. The Arizona desert was crawling with would-be gold miners recently arrived from the East with high expectations of finding their fortunes in the mineral wealth of the Southwest. When they arrived, they bought good animals and the necessary camping and prospecting equipment to facilitate their search for riches. After searching in the mountains and deserts along the Mexican border for several months and finding nothing of value, many of them would return to Tucson defeated and ready to catch the first train back to their homes in the East. By that time, the animals were exhausted and under-nourished and their equipment mostly dull, dirty, or worn-out. Jeff would buy the whole outfit for pennies on the dollar, clean-up and salvage what equipment could be saved, rest, comb, and feed the animals, and sell the whole works to the next fortune seeker just arrived from the East at a nice profit. He wasn't getting rich, but he was making a living. He supplemented his income from time to time by guiding parties of hunters and prospectors into the surround desert and sometimes into Mexico.

He also seems to have for the first time enjoyed a rather active social life. He didn't have a steady girlfriend, but he was often seen around town escorting one or another of Tucson's finer unattached young ladies.

Jeff Milton is often described as having been stern and laconic to a fault, even to the point of rudeness on occasion, but that's not completely accurate. If he had something to say, he didn't beat about the bush; he came right to the point, and he didn't mince words. Everyone knew exactly where they stood in the scheme of things with him, and there was generally little room for negotiation and compromise. It is probably true that in the company of people that he didn't know well, he was quiet and somewhat reserved, but people who knew him well say that in the right circumstances, *he could talk an arm off you!* He seems to have liked to keep his distance, and few men ever got really close to him. Nevertheless, even those who didn't like him respected him, and he made a lot of casual friends wherever he went.

A horse fell with Jeff and broke his ankle in January of 1890. The bone would probably have healed faster had he done what his doctor told him to do and stayed off that leg to give it time to heal, but, true to his nature, Jeff paid no attention to the doctor's instructions. Within a few days, he was up hobbling around town on his crutches. Two weeks later, he made a horseback trip to Mexico with his leg bound up in a splint and the padding saturated with horse liniment to kill the pain. That bit of foolishness apparently made a believer of him, and when he returned to Tucson he curtailed his physical activities and followed his doctor's orders until the leg healed.

With nothing else to do, he threw his hat into the political ring. He stood for county tax assessor. Jeff obviously wasn't a politician. He wasn't devious by nature, and he didn't know how the political game was played. He lost the election, embarrassingly so. From that day forward, he had no use for politicians, and he would never again run for public office.

Taking it easy may have been good for his broken ankle, but limiting his activity and eating most of his meals in restaurants put weight on him, lots of weight. " I was too big to be a man and not big enough to be a horse, and I was broke," he later told J. Evetts Haley.

Jeff was again in need of a job, and he decided that he wanted to be a railroad man. He had no previous experience of any kind on the railroad, and, of course, he had to start at the bottom. He went to work on the Texas and Pacific Railroad as a fireman. Flabby and out of shape from the long period of convalescence, the hours of shoveling coal into the steam engine's boiler were torture. After the first trip, he was sore in every joint and every muscle in his body, but he refused to quit. He stuck to it, and the work got easier and easier as time passed. The extra pounds melted away and the soreness went with them.

His work as a fireman on the Texas and Pacific took him to El Paso frequently, and on one of his trips, he met the Superintendent of the Pullman Company. He was impressed with Jeff, and he offered him a job as a Pullman conductor on the Mexican railroad line from El Paso to Mexico City. It would be a lot less strenuous, and it paid considerably more money. Jeff jumped at it.

By the summer of 1894, Jeff Milton was well known by the movers and shakers of El Paso city government; those who didn't know him personally knew him by reputation. El Paso was a wide open city, the liquor flowed freely and gambling and prostitution in the saloons and bawdy houses was unbridled. This, of course, made the city attractive to the lower elements of society, and some of the toughest outlaws and gunslingers in the West congregated in El Paso. Lawlessness was out-of-hand. The city fathers decided that something had to be done about it, but who could police such a town? There weren't many who would take on the job and fewer still that could be relied upon to do it properly. The mayor and several others suggested Jeff Milton, and he was offered the position of Chief of Police.

Jeff wasn't sure that he wanted the job. El Paso had been through these *reform* movements before. They usually didn't last very long, only until the crackdown began to affect the financial interests of the local politicians; the mayor and several of the city councilmen had financial interests in the saloons. After thinking about it for a few days, he accepted the position; although, he still had reservations. He was sworn in as Chief of Police of the City of El Paso on August 10, 1894.

As a first step, Jeff fired most of the city policemen, those that he considered inept or corrupt or a combination of inept and corrupt, and he replaced them with men of his own choosing. Then he set about making the point with the local *bad men*: He had been appointed to enforce the law and to keep the peace, and he intended to do just that. Perhaps because of his reputation, or perhaps it was his approach, he generally got his point across without having to resort to violence. Nevertheless, everyone in town knew that he was perfectly capable and willing to use his weapons, his big fists, and a booted foot when the circumstances made it necessary.

John Selman, a particularly perverted gunman who had killed more than thirty men, most of them murdered in cold blood, was constable of the first precinct in El Paso when Jeff became Chief of Police. Jeff couldn't get rid of him, but he let him know in no uncertain terms that his days were numbered if he didn't behave himself. His second day on the job, Jeff caught Selman's deputy constable collecting money from prostitutes for *protection*. He arrested the man and threw him in jail. Selman ranted and raved, but he knew better than to interfere.

Jeff didn't like John Selman, and he intended to *get him* at the first opportunity, but in spite of that, he hired Selman's son as a policeman, not visiting the sins of the father on the son. It was just another example of the principles that Jeff Milton seems to have lived by all of his life; he was tough, and he could be mean and dangerous in a fight, but he always tried to be fair.

John Wesley Hardin, a psychopathic killer with twenty some dead men behind him, was practicing law in El Paso, and he was used to doing as he pleased. He was known as the deadliest and meanest gunfighter in Texas at the time, and no policeman in El Paso had dared to approach him for any reason. Jeff came upon him and two friends drinking in a saloon one evening. Each of the three was carrying a six-shooter in violation of a city ordinance. Jeff disarmed the three politely but firmly, and he gave Hardin the same unmistakable message that he had given to Selman.

A week after Jeff Milton was appointed Chief of Police, the El Paso City Council revoked all previously issued gambling permits and passed an ordinance prohibiting gambling within the city. Jeff compiled a list of all the known *tinhorns* in town, and he began serving notice on them to leave town or be arrested. Most of them left; the few who decided to challenge the Chief of Police found themselves sitting in the El Paso *juzgado*.

He served notice on the owners of all of the gambling establishments within the city that they were closed indefinitely. If they chose to continue operating, they would be arrested. A few chose to ignore his advice, and they continued their gambling, and a few others chose to threaten him with physical violence or political retribution if he interfered with their operations. He refused to be swayed, and within a few days all of the gambling establishments in El Paso were closed, and a few of the owners were keeping the *tinhorns* company in the city jail.

Jeff did what he was hired to do, but he didn't always play by the strict rules of law and procedure. He sometimes enforced laws that didn't exist, because he thought that it was *the right thing to do*. On other occasions he ignored obvious violations of the law when it suited him to do so. In the circumstances that existed in El Paso at that time, it was probably the only way that he could have handled the job, but it didn't make everybody happy. You just can't please everybody all the time.

As Jeff had predicted when he took the job, El Paso wouldn't tolerate *reform* for long. Robert F. Campbell, better known as *Poker Bob*, was elected mayor on April 9, 1895. The *reform* ordinances were repealed almost immediately, the gambling halls reopened, and Chief of Police Jefferson Davis Milton was dismissed.

After his somewhat short tenure with the City of El Paso, Jeff was appointed a Deputy U.S. Marshal, and he also accepted a commission as a Special Texas Ranger. He and his old friend from Ranger days, George Scarborough, transported federal prisoners as far as Detroit, Michigan, and they filled their spare time participating in several manhunts in West Texas and New Mexico.

It was about this time that John Selman murdered Texas Ranger Bass Outlaw and John Wesley Hardin in El Paso, and then he tried to ambush George Scarborough, but that didn't work out as he had planned. The federal marshal put an end to Selman's violent career once and for all. Jeff Milton would tell friends in later years that he always regretted not having killed John Selman the first time he met him.

Jeff was content being a deputy marshal and a Special Texas Ranger, but the pay for both jobs was poor and he was looking for something better. While he was Chief of Police in El Paso the Southern Pacific Railroad agent had offered him a hundred dollars a month for *special protection* of railroad property in the city. Jeff had refused to accept the money, saying that the city already paid him for that. He made an impression on the railroad man; honest, reliable, and capable men were not easy to find in the West in those days. So when Wells-Fargo had a large shipment of gold going to San Francisco, he thought of Jeff Milton, and Jeff went to work for Wells-Fargo as a messenger and guard. After he finished that assignment, he was given a permanent job as a combined express agent and guard on the run from Benson, Arizona, through Nogales to Guaymas, Sonora, Mexico.

Jeff spent the next three years riding the rails between Benson and Guaymas in an express car, loading and unloading freight, and chasing thieves on horseback, some of whom were the most dangerous and desperate criminals of their time, through the deserts and mountains of Southern Arizona and Northern Mexico. Sometimes he was alone; sometimes he was accompanied by his good friend and colleague George Scarborough, and sometimes he was accompanied by the famous Mexican Colonel Emilio Kosterlitzky, *Comandante de los Rurales*, in Sonora, who also became a close and loyal friend. In return for all of this, he was paid the handsome sum of eighty-five dollars a month by Wells-Fargo and Company. The pay wasn't great, but he liked what he was doing; money had never been most important to him. It was enough that he enjoyed what he was doing, but it would all come to an end on the night of February 15, 1900.

It was supposed to have been Jeff's day-off, and he should have left the train at Nogales, but his relief was sick and Jeff stayed on the job. The train pulled into the station at Fairbank, about fifteen miles west of Tombstone, just about dusk. There was the usual small crowd of people waiting at the station, freighters, railroad employees, and people waiting to board the train or waiting for passengers arriving on the train. Jeff was in the express car getting his mail and deliveries for Fairbank and Tombstone ready to drop off. Suddenly, he heard a commotion outside, and he opened the sliding door of the express car to see what was going on. He was confronted by five masked men armed with rifles; they were obviously intent on robbing the express car.

"Throw up your hands and come out o' there," came a command, then a shot, and Jeff's hat flew off.

"If there's anything here you want, come and get it," Jeff replied, as he reached for his shotgun. Unfortunately, he couldn't shoot at the bandits without the chance of hitting innocent people in the crowd.

He started to close the sliding door, and the bandits opened fire all together. He was hit in the left arm between the elbow and the shoulder, and the bullet shattered the bone. He fell on his back between boxes of freight, and he lost consciousness for a minute or two. When he regained his senses, he realized that he was badly injured and unable to regain his feet. He knew what the bandits were after; the safe was full of cash and gold. He took the keys to the safe out of his pocket and threw them into a pile of packages, hoping that the bandits wouldn't be able to find them, and he passed-out again.

The bandits did get into the freight car, and they searched the car and Jeff's pockets for the keys to the safe, but they didn't find them. Unable to open the safe and unable to carry it off with them, they left with nothing for all their trouble. These were not the brightest bandits in the West, and they were all later caught, but that's another story.

Jeff was rushed to Benson and then on to Tucson by train. Doctor Fenner was waiting at St. Mary's Hospital in Tucson when he arrived. His injuries were beyond the doctor's competence, but he did what he could. He tried to repair the damage to the bone in Jeff's upper left arm with piano wire and then bound the whole arm tightly with cotton bandages. Jeff was in excruciating pain, and the wound wouldn't heal properly. Over the next several weeks his condition worsened, and Wells-Fargo arranged for him to go to the Southern Pacific Hospital in San Francisco.

Jeff remained at the Southern Pacific Hospital for eight months. He underwent several procedures there, but still the arm was not healing as it should. Finally, the doctors gave up. They decided that they would have to amputate the arm at the shoulder; the wound was beginning to putrefy and it was just a matter of time until gangrene would set in and threaten Jeff's life.

When Jeff was told of the doctors' plans, he absolutely refused. He would *not* let them take his arm, and he checked himself out of the hospital against the doctor's advice that day.

Doctor George A. Goodfellow, the well-known physician credited with saving so many lives in Tombstone's heyday, had moved to San Francisco and become a renowned surgeon. Jeff had known Doctor Goodfellow in Tombstone, and he had a high opinion of the doctor's competence. He had a friend take him to the Lane Hospital, where Doctor Goodfellow was practicing, and he asked the doctor to take a look at his arm.

Doctor Goodfellow cut away all of the putrefying tissue and removed all of the piano wire and about three inches of bone from Jeff's upper arm. Jeff was in excruciating pain for a week or more, but then the pain eased as the wound healed. In about a month he had recovered sufficiently for him to leave the hospital.

Doctor Goodfellow made a leather brace to support Jeff's arm and sent him on his way. The arm hung useless at his side. "You'll never be able to use that arm for anything, but at least you still have most of it," he told Jeff.

Jeff wouldn't accept the complete loss of the use of his arm, and he forced himself to move fingers slightly and then the hand. Gradually, he built up strength in the crippled arm to the point where he could move it, but for the most part, the doctor was right, the arm was useless.

While he was convalescing in San Francisco, Jeff had a lot of time to read newspapers and magazines. For the first time, he began to take notice of what was going on in the country as a whole. People were getting rich in the oil business, which was booming in Texas. He had saved a little money while he was working for Wells-Fargo, and the company had given him a healthy bonus for saving the cash and gold in the safe from the bandits at Fairbank. Since his career as a lawman had apparently come to an end with the loss of his arm; he might as well go back to Texas and get rich in the oil business, he thought.

The J.D. Milton Oil Company of Houston, Texas, was basically a one-man operation. It was never well-capitalized, and it lacked management and technical talent, as well, but it was never lacking in enthusiasm. Jeff acquired some oil leases, and he hired a drilling crew, and they proceeded to punch holes in the Texas prairie for the next two years. When his money ran out, all he had to show for it was a collection of dry holes and worn-out drilling tools.

Jeff wasn't ready to give up on the oil business, though. Oil had been discovered in California, and he had some wealthy friends there. In just a few weeks, he managed to raise enough money to finance a prospecting venture in Mexico, and he set-out with typical enthusiasm.

Although Jeff seems to have had a *very good time* running around from one end of Mexico to the other in search of oil and mineral deposits, he didn't find anything of much value, and his backers finally cut him off. He returned to Arizona in the spring of 1904, nearly broke and again in need of a job.

Congress established a separate Bureau of Immigration in 1885, which slowly opened offices at various places around the United States and assigned *Immigrant Inspectors* at larger and busier ports of entry to examine arriving immigrants, but Customs officers continued to enforce the immigration laws at the smaller ports of entry and on the border between the ports of entry. Then the Immigration Service in the Department of Commerce and Labor was created in 1903 and assumed jurisdiction of immigration enforcement throughout the United States.

It soon came to someone's attention in the new Service that the smuggling of Chinese across the Mexican border was a widespread practice, and no one had thought to provide for enforcement of the immigration laws along the Mexican border between the ports of entry now that the Customs Service was out of the immigration business.

The official title of the position created within the Immigration Service in 1903 was *Mounted Border Guard*, but they were often referred to as *Chinese Immigration Inspectors*, probably out of confusion with the title of the Customs officers who had previously enforced the Chinese Exclusion Law.

Jeff Milton was appointed a Mounted Border Guard in Tucson, Arizona, in May of 1904. There is confusion over just how he happened to get the job, but *my* best guess is that he was probably recommended by Customs officers and other prominent people in the area who knew him, liked him, and respected him. He had been a Mounted Customs Inspector, deputy U.S. Marshal, railroad employee, businessman, and Wells-Fargo employee in the area for several years, and he was well-acquainted. That makes a lot more sense than the sometimes told and occasionally printed tale that President Theodore Roosevelt created this unique and singular position in government service especially for his dear friend, Jefferson Davis Milton.

Jeff's salary as a Mounted Border Guard in 1904 was five dollars a day, plus an additional three dollars and fifty cents a day subsistence. It amounted to just fifty cents a day more than what Customs Chinese Exclusion Officers were paid in salary and subsistence ten years earlier.

It's often been said that Jeff Milton was the *first* immigration border patrol officer, and that he occupied the only such position in the Immigration Service at the time. He was surely among the first, but I don't believe that he was the first and only. It's probable that there were others appointed ahead of him or at about the same time. His friend and colleague, Sam Webb, with whom he patrolled the border in Arizona for several years, was employed by the Immigration Service as an Immigrant Inspector before he became a Mounted Border Guard, and I suspect that he was appointed before Jeff. And there were other Mounted Border Guards appointed in El Paso and Brownsville, Texas, and possibly at other places on the border, at about the same time. Who was first, second, third, is impossible to determine at this late date, and it doesn't make a helluva lot of difference, anyway.

The Courthouse Museum in Tombstone, Arizona, has on display, along with one of Jeff Milton's rifles, some photographs, and a few other things that belonged to him, a badge purportedly worn by Jeff as a Mounted Border Guard. A printed card in front of the badge states: *The first Immigration and Naturalization Service badge. Because Milton was the first immigration officer appointed, this is the first badge ever issued.* I don't know who made the card, but it is, of course, not accurate.

I tried to find out where the badge came from, but no one that I talked to was sure of its origin. The museum manager told me that the card was made before he came to the museum. He didn't know who made it or where they got their information, and he too questioned the accuracy of the information on the card. He was sure, however, that the badge did belong to Jeff Milton at some point in his life, as it is listed with the other items *on loan* to the museum from surviving family members living in Texas.

The badge is a rather crude thing, by today's standards, and I've never seen another like it anywhere. It appears to be made from the eagle crest of a turn-of-the-century U.S. Army officer's cap device with a banner containing the letters U.S.I.S. soldered between the tips of the eagle's wings.

It's possible that the Mounted Border Guards didn't have a unique badge, and this *unofficial* badge was made specifically for Jeff Milton. It appears to have been hand crafted. When I tried to pursue that possibility, I was told by one Tombstone *historian* that the badge was made by a Tombstone gunsmith. Another *historian* on the same day told me that it was made by a blacksmith at Fort Huachuca. If I had talked to a third *historian*, I have no doubt that I would have been told another story.

Jeff's position description, which contained broad statements such as,*...entirely upon his own initiative and responsibility*...and *...under the supervision of the Commissioner General of Immigration...*, has led some writers to believe that Jeff was on his own, free to roam where he pleased, when he pleased, and do as he pleased, without regard to field office supervisors of the fledgling Immigration Service. That is definitely not true. He operated directly under the supervision of the Immigrant Inspector-in-Charge at Tucson, but at various times there were one or more supervisors between him and the Immigrant Inspector-in-Charge. They determined where he would patrol and how he would patrol the border, and Jeff found himself under closer supervision than he had been as a Mounted Customs Inspector.

It was made clear to Jeff and the other Mounted Border Guards that they would patrol *exclusively* the area assigned to them, and they would patrol *exclusively* on the *north* side of the line; excursions across the border into Mexico were permitted only for intelligence and liaison purposes, brief meetings with informants and Mexican officials. They were also required to send the supervisor frequent and detailed written activity reports.

In the beginning, Jeff chafed under the restrictions, and he didn't pay much attention to the details, especially those involving reporting and record keeping. He had always had an independent streak, and he was used to doing as he pleased. He sometimes wandered out of his assigned patrol area, and he took a rather lackadaisical attitude toward his reports; if he had nothing significant to report, he simply skipped sending a report. Had it not been for his reputation as a conscientious lawman and his friends in the Service, he would have lost his job in the first year; he came close more than once. He wasn't happy with the circumstances, but he gradually realized that he was going to have to comply with orders or find another job. He liked his job and he didn't want to lose it, so he quit fighting the system.

In the beginning, the only immigration laws being enforced were those baring Chinese from the country, but as the years passed and the immigration laws evolved and they assumed more responsibility, the Mounted Border Guard title was changed to Immigrant Inspector.

Jeff patrolled mainly in the San Pedro Valley from Tombstone and Fairbank, but he was frequently sent to other places on temporary assignments at the whim of his supervisor in Tucson. He settled into the routine, and he was soon considered to be an excellent and productive officer. When he was told to move, he would pack up his belongings and move to a new base camp without complaint. It was all part of the job.

In the spring of 1918, Jeff was sent to Indian Oasis, on the Papago Indian Reservation Southwest of Tucson, on a semi-permanent assignment. Indian Oasis has since changed it's name, and it is now known as Sells, Arizona. It was a move that would change his life in ways that he would never have imagined.

Mildred Taitt, a forty year old school teacher from Gouverneur, New York, a small community on the Canadian border, on sabbatical studying at the University of Arizona in Tucson in the spring of 1919. She was visiting friends, Presbyterian missionaries, at Indian Oasis, when she chanced to meet Jefferson Davis Milton. Perhaps, the old proverb that opposites attract is true; two people could not have been more different. He was a big, tough, robust frontiersman. Mildred was a slight, gentle woman, less than half his size, in poor health. She was an educated woman, a college graduate. Jeff was not illiterate, but his speech and his manners were far from polished. He was an unrepentant and unapologetic Southerner, a Democrat to the core. Mildred was a *Yankee* Republican. It seems that they had little or nothing in common. Nevertheless, they were married June 30, 1919, less than six months after they met for the first time, and Mildred moved to Indian Oasis to begin her new life. She was forty years old; Jeff was fifty-seven, and neither had been previously married. None of his friends nor any of her friends could understand it. Could this be love? Whatever it was, it was real; they remained devoted to each other for almost thirty years.

The automobile had found its way into the Immigration Service in 1918, and Jeff was doing a lot of his traveling in a stripped down Model T Ford. It couldn't replace a horse in the rough country along the border, of course, but it shortened the trips between towns considerably. Jeff loved his horses, but he liked roaring around at breakneck speeds of almost thirty miles an hour in the government automobile, too.

In October of that year, Jeff was transferred back to the San Pedro River Valley, and he and his wife loaded all of their worldly possessions into the Model T and moved to Fairbank. It couldn't have been an easy life for her, but Mildred took it in stride. She was one of the first of the Border Patrol wives to begin the long tradition of following their men from one desolate duty station to the next, and she set a fine example for all of those who would follow.

The United States Border Patrol was born on May 28, 1924, a separate unit of the Immigration Service within the Department of Labor. A force of four hundred fifty men was initially authorized. The Mounted Border Guards at the time numbered about seventy-five men, and almost all of them were absorbed into the new Border Patrol. Over the next several months, former sheriffs, Texas Rangers, and a number of men who were on a civil service register waiting for jobs as railroad mail clerks were hired to fill-out the ranks of the Border Patrol.

New *Patrol Inspectors*, as they were now designated, were paid a starting salary of $1,680 a year. They were issued a badge and a revolver - uniforms would not adopted until late in 1932. Each Patrol Inspector was required to furnish his own horse and saddle and whatever other equipment that he needed. A formal training school for new recruits would not begin until 1934. In the mean time, the new men learned on-the-job from the old-timers, and they were taught well.

Jeff Milton was sixty-two years old when the Border Patrol was established, and there was talk of not taking him into the new agency because of his age and his crippled left arm. Such talk was quickly put to rest when George J. Harris, Assistant Commissioner of Immigration, wrote of him: *He is simply a wonder when it comes to physical endurance, activity, and value to the Service. All of his life he has been an outdoor man, a Texas Ranger, Chief of Police, Customs officer, etc. He is a fearless, active, resourceful man with a host of friends ever ready to give him information or otherwise assist him. He is invaluable to this service, and barring unforeseen accidents or illnesses, is likely to continue so right up to the maximum age of 70.*

Jeff continued to patrol the border. When he reached the age of seventy, the age for mandatory retirement at the time, he was still going strong. He was granted a waiver of the maximum age limit for two years, but an economy measure in the Service forced his retirement on June 30, 1932, a few months short of his seventy-second birthday. He was given a pension of one hundred dollars a month.

In a lifetime of enforcing the law in wild and dangerous country, Jeff Milton no doubt upset some people, and he made some enemies. His detractors have said that he was nothing but a gunman, a paid *killer*. It's true that he did kill some men. The exact number may never be known, but it's probably fewer than have been credited to him. As he explained to J. Evetts Haley, "I never killed a man that didn't need killing, and I never shot an animal except for meat." I believe him. Jeff Milton was far more than a hired gunman.

At the time of his retirement, Jeff and Mildred were living in Tombstone, and they remained there in retirement for many years. Their home on Second Street a couple of blocks north of the Courthouse Museum stands today much as it did when they lived there. It is occupied by the current owner and is not open to the public; however, a prominent historical marker on a post in front of the house identifies it as *The Milton House.*

Jeff was restless in retirement, and he often went on camping trips out into the desert. Sometimes he went alone, and sometimes Mildred or friends would accompany him. In later years, Border Patrol officers would occasionally stop by and he would ride-along on patrol with them. As he got older and had trouble getting around by himself, Border Patrol officers would take him where he needed to go and then return him to his home.

Gene Pyeatt, who retired from the INS as a Supervisory Criminal Investigator in Los Angeles, California, lived in Tombstone as a child. He remembers Jeff and Mildred Milton well, as he passed their home on his way to school everyday. He recalls them as quiet, but friendly and gracious people. When Gene joined the Border Patrol in 1950, he received a card in the mail from Mrs. Milton; the card read simply: "He would be proud of you." He saved the card for years.

When Jeff's health started failing, he and Mildred moved to Tucson, where they were looked over by Border Patrol friends. When it became apparent that the end was near, Border Patrol officers Gordon Pettingill, Bob Jarratt, Phil Walker, and Ed Egan took turns sitting with him in shifts. Ed Egan recalls that Bob

Jarratt was with him when he died on May 7, 1947. All of these officers who sat with him during his last hours went on to retire from the INS in high level management positions.

J. Evetts Haley, Jeff's biographer and perhaps the man who knew him best at the end of his life, gave the eulogy at his funeral. Following the funeral, his body was cremated and the ashes scattered over the Arizona desert that he loved so much in accordance with his wishes.

\+ \+ \+ \+ \+ \+ \+

Note: For a more detailed account of the life of Jefferson Davis Milton, see: *Jeff Milton, A Good Man With A Gun*, by J. Evetts Haley, University of Oklahoma Press, 1948, from which much of the information in this article was derived. Our thanks to the J. Evetts Haley Estate and J. Evetts Haley, Jr. of Midland, Texas, for approving our use of the passages we have reprinted here. GB

Big Game Hunting
by
Orville Lewis

Several years after the United States and Mexico set the International Boundary between Mexico and Texas at the Rio Grande River, the river changed it's course and left a small piece of land, slightly more than a square mile, bordered on three sides by the United States and on one side by Mexico. It was called Cordova Island, and in it's southeast corner there was a row of houses facing north with their backyards extending to the International Boundary. It was fairly easy for illegal aliens to cross the border into the backyards without being seen, so for that reason we regularly patrolled the street in front of the houses.

At one of the houses there lived a brute of a dog, and this man-eater just loved to chase motor vehicles, any kind of motor vehicles, cars, trucks, jeeps, what-have-you. It made no difference to him; he'd come charging out snarling and barking his fool head off. This had been going on for several months; it was a real nuisance, but the dog had never bitten anyone, and there wasn't anything that we could do about him.

I sat in a patrol car at the end of the street one afternoon for well more than an hour and watched this goofy animal wander around in front of his owner's house apparently oblivious to the world around him. Car after car, truck after truck, there might even have been a school bus or two, passed the house, and Fido ignored them all. However, when I decided to move, and I drove the marked Border Patrol jeep in front of the house, he came running out snarling and barking as though he intended to eat me alive. Hey! I thought. He only chases Border Patrol vehicles. That's discrimination! It was time something was done about Fido, and I was just the man to do it. But what could I do? I didn't want to hurt somebody's pet.

About a week later, I was working the four to midnight shift. Bill Joyner was the supervisor, and Bill and I were friends. We had worked together at the Border Patrol Academy where Bill was a firearms instructor. I'd seen him on several occasions putting on shooting demonstrations for trainees using blank cartridges that he made up himself with only a primer cap and a small wax plug in the open end of an empty brass cartridge case. When they were fired in a pistol, they made a fairly loud *pop* sound and the wax plug would travel six feet or so from the end of the gun barrel. The wax plug might sting a bit if it hit you on bare skin, but it couldn't actually hurt anyone. That gave me an idea of how to deal with my canine nemesis.

I told Bill about the dog, and I asked him to give me one of his training cartridges. I thought that maybe a little *pop* and a sting on his butt might break this hound of his dangerous game. Besides, I resented his only chasing Border Patrol vehicles, and a little bang on the butt might teach him some manners.

The next afternoon when I started my shift Bill handed me one of his training cartridges. I checked it over and made sure that the bullet was just wax, and then I slipped it into my shirt pocket.

It was just before midnight when my partner and I decided to make a pass by the houses on Cordova Island where Fido undoubtedly would be waiting to ambush us. I asked my partner to drive slowly, and I emptied my revolver and loaded the one training cartridge. As we approached the house, Fido came charging out, right on cue. I leaned out, pointed my pistol at his flanks, and pulled the trigger.

I don't know who got the greater shock, Fido or me. The pistol didn't *pop* as I was expecting; it erupted with a ***Booooom!!!*** probably heard for several city blocks. Flame shot out of the end of the barrel for about five feet. That damn Bill Joyner had filled the cartridge case with smokeless powder before he capped it with wax.

Lights started coming on in houses up and down the street. "Let's get the hell out of here!" I shouted at my partner, and we departed from Cordova Island in a hurry.

So far as I know, that dog never again chased a Border Patrol vehicle.

\+ + + + + + +

The Best Job We Ever Had

by

Walt Edwards

I started in the Border Patrol at El Paso, Texas, in May of 1951. It was a different organization than it is today; there was no such thing as a *union*, and all of the civil service protections didn't necessarily apply to *temporary conditional* appointees. The *conditional* part meant that you behaved yourself, paid attention to instructions, and did as you were told. *Probies*, as trainee Patrol Inspectors were known in those days, had few employment rights, and they virtually belonged to the sector Chief Patrol Inspector. The chiefs had the authority to terminate probationary employees almost at whim. You behaved yourself, worked hard, and did as you were told, or you were soon gone.

I'd only been there a few days when I and several other *probies* were assigned to a work detail tearing out the radio room on the first floor of the sector headquarters building at old Camp Chigas and moving everything to the second floor. It was basically construction labor, dirty and unpleasant, and all of us were grumbling about that not being the kind of work we had joined the Border Patrol to do. I was careful not to grumble too loud or anywhere that I might be overheard. The Border Patrol was the best job that I'd ever had or was likely to get anytime in the immediate future, and I wasn't about to put my job at risk.

The griping and grumbling was understandable; we all wanted to be out on the border chasing *Juan Mojado*, and we thought that the badge alone fully qualified us to *get on with it*! We really had very little understanding of what the job was all about. We never considered how dangerous turning us loose at that time would be, not only for us, but for *Juan Mojado* and anyone else who might have been in the neighborhood, as well. We had no idea of the limitations on our authority as immigration officers, and most of us spoke little or no Spanish. John Robert Cain, the sector training officer, took us out to the city dump and showed us which end of the pistol the bullet came out of, and that was about the extent of our training up to that point.

Before I joined the Border Patrol, I'd worked for the Veterans Administration as an X-Ray technician for about three years, and I knew a little about civil service regulations. I knew, for instance, that if I worked on a holiday, I would be entitled to overtime pay, and I was in bad need of money. The day before Memorial Day, I was dutifully pulling nails and rebuilding the radio console when John P. Swanson, who was then the Assistant Chief Patrol Inspector, walked by. I almost jumped to attention to speak to him, and I asked, "Mr. Swanson, do you want me to work in here tomorrow?"

He gave me a hard look, his moustache twitched, and I thought for a moment that I could see steam coming out of his ears. "Yes, I want you to work in here tomorrow!," he said. "And I don't want to hear any more bitchin' about this work detail!" With that, he turned on his heel and walked away. I went back to work.

I reported for duty at 7:00 A.M. on Memorial Day, picked up my hammer, and went to work. I was the only *probie* there.

About nine o'clock that morning, Mr. Swanson came in, and he saw me working away. He said, "What in hell are you doing here? Don't you know this is a holiday?" I reminded him that we had discussed it the day before, and that he had instructed me to come to work. The mustache twisted into a grin, and he said, "Go ahead, get back to work, then." I finished out the day, and a couple weeks later, I collected the overtime pay. As I said, I needed the money. The starting salary back then was $3,450 a year, and it was six weeks before we got the first paycheck. Most of us were broke and borrowing before that first check arrived.

I stayed on the work detail in El Paso for about three weeks, and then I was transferred to Las Cruces, New Mexico. The Border Patrol Training School, as it was called then, was on the campus of New Mexico A .& M. College, and I thought I'd be attending the next class, but no such luck. Apparently, someone liked my remodeling work at sector headquarters, and I'd been transferred to Las Cruces to do some renovation on the buildings at the college that were to be used for Border Patrol training.

A few weeks later, I finished the Las Cruces job to the satisfaction of Henry Blackwell, the director of the training school, and I was finally allowed to do some actual border patrolling with the officers in the

Las Cruces station. It was about time!

I made some good friends in the Las Cruces station. Darrell Warren sort of took me under his wing, and he and his wife, Doris, were just great to me. Fourteen years later, Darrell and I would again work together as Investigators in Dallas. Even ol' Robert St. Clair, who hated working with probationers and often went a whole shift without uttering ten words to his partner, came to tolerate working with me.

I continued working with the officers in Las Cruces until I went to the forty-fifth session of the Border Patrol Training School. We graduated the middle of September, and I was immediately reassigned to Presidio, Texas. My buddy, Ray Morris, and I drove all night from Las Cruces to Presidio in my car. It's mighty hot in the daytime in West Texas in September, and it was more comfortable to travel at night in those days before automobile air conditioning. Besides, we weren't sure that my old 1940 Dodge would make the trip in the heat of the day.

When I reported in at Presidio, Cal Darst was the station senior, and Roger Bushner was his *segundo*. They were both good at their jobs. They were fair and well liked by their men, but they ran a tight operation. It was evident right from the start that they weren't going to put up with a lot of foolishness.

Presidio was considered tough duty, and there weren't a lot of journeymen officers who wanted to go there. As a result, there were more probationers than journeymen, and the more senior probationers were being scheduled to work together as partners. That's how I happened to be working with Jay Ailshie in the winter of 1951. He was what we called a *retread*; he had been in a previous class, and he failed to complete probation. He had been terminated for some reason, but later on someone decided to give him a second chance. He was rehired, and he was then going through training again with our class.

It was late in the afternoon, and Jay and I were working down river from Presidio toward Redford. We had information that a previous deportee had returned to the United States illegally and was working on a farm near the river. He was supposed to be living in an old adobe house on the farm. Both Jay and I were fairly familiar with the area, and we knew where the house was located. We also knew that the local *grapevine* was such that our alien would be warned of our presence in the area and be long gone by the time that we reached the adobe house in our Border Patrol Jeep.

Jay was driving, and we decided that I would drop out of the Jeep on the roll as Jay shifted gears when we crossed through an arroyo. Hopefully, I wouldn't be seen by anyone, and I could make my way unseen through the brush and trees to a position behind the house. Jay would wait until after dark, and then he would drive up to the front of the house with the headlights on and *flush* the alien out of the house. We expected him to run out the back where I could grab him. It seemed like a good plan, so when we crossed through the arroyo, I bailed out of the Jeep.

About a half mile from the house I ran into a man in a thicket of salt-cedar. He admitted that he was an alien, but he claimed to have a *permiso*. He said that he was an informant for Cal Darst. He didn't have the *permiso* with him, and I wasn't going to take his word for it. I planned to take him back to the station, and if he was telling the truth, I'd release him. However, at the moment, I had more pressing business to attend to. I took him into a plowed field, handcuffed his left wrist to his right ankle, and jokingly told him not to run away. I thought about handcuffing him to one of the trees, but it was beginning to get dark, and I was in a hurry to get to my post behind the old adobe house where our previously deported alien was supposed to be living.

I got into a position behind the house just before dark, and I waited for Jay to *flush* our man out of the house into my arms. Then I waited some more. There wasn't much cover behind the house, and when the full moon came up, I felt as though it was a spotlight pointed directly at me. After about an hour, I realized that something had gone wrong and Jay wasn't coming. I decided to pick up my handcuffed alien and walk him back out to the river road. Hopefully, Jay would meet us there.

When I returned to the spot where I'd left the alien, he wasn't there. I called to him softly, but I got no response. Then I called to him not quite so softly, and I still got no response. Then I whistled loudly…. no response. Then I got mad and threatened him at the top of my voice with all sorts of dire consequences if he didn't answer me. I still got no response. The moonlight was so bright by then that I could see almost the whole plowed field ….nothing. I switched on my flashlight and played the beam across the ground. His tracks were clearly visible in the freshly turned soil; they were going straight toward the Rio Grande.

I began tracking him - left footprint - right kneeprint - left footprint - right kneeprint, and so on. The tracks were easy to follow, and I was moving much faster than he could with his wrist handcuffed to his ankle, but I didn't know when he started moving. He could have as much as an hour head start on me. He could have possibly made it to the river, but he surely couldn't swim across, handcuffed as he was. Oh Lord! I thought. What if he tried to swim across the river and drowned? I began to worry, and I started moving faster following his tracks.

I lost the alien's tracks in the grass at the river's edge. It seemed certain that he had gone into the water. What should I do? I started to plead with the alien on the off chance that he was hiding somewhere within hearing. "Hey, amigo! I believe that you're Mr. Darst's informant," I shouted. "I'll let you go! I'll take the handcuffs off, and you can go on your way." There was no response. It was a cool night, but I was beginning to sweat. My imagination was running wild, and I could picture his lifeless body floating down the river.

About this time, a pair of headlights came into view on the river road. It was Jay coming back in the Border Patrol Jeep. I flagged him down with my flashlight.

"Where in hell have you been?" I shouted when he stopped the Jeep in front of me. He said that he'd gotten lost trying to find the road to the adobe house, and he had just found his way back to the river road. I told him about the alien I'd caught and handcuffed, and that I feared he might have tried to cross the river and drowned.

"You better not tell the *jefes* that you had him handcuffed that way," Jay advised. "Man, they'll fire you in a New York minute! Maybe, you should tell them that you were crawling through the brush and lost your cuffs out of the case."

"Oh, yeah! That's a great idea," I said. "Let's lie about it! And then when his body washes up on the riverbank with my handcuffs on him, what am I going to say? How am I going to explain that?"

Jay came back with some dumb remark, "Your funeral," or something like that. I let it go, but I was beginning to understand why he had failed probation the first time around.

We looked for a couple of hours for the alien or any sign of him, but we couldn't find anything in the dark. We got back in the Jeep and drove back to the station. There was nothing left for me to do but face the music…. and perhaps pack my bags. I fully expected to be unemployed by the end of the week.

It was still fairly early in the evening, and after I dropped Jay at the station, I went to Roger Bushner's home to tell him what had happened. Somehow, telling the *segundo* my sad tale didn't seem to be quite so hard as confessing to Cal Darst. I told it all, every detail, including how I'd handcuffed the alien's wrist to his ankle, and that I feared that he had drowned because he couldn't swim the way I'd handcuffed him.

Bush stuffed a dip of Copenhagen in his mouth, leaned back in his chair, and *allowed as to how* the world had not yet come to an end. He suggested that we go to the station and pick up a piece of *high-tech* equipment he had there, and then we'd go back down to the river together and see what we could find.

The *high-tech* equipment turned out to be a six-volt automobile battery in a metal box, an extension cord, and a spotlight. I don't remember exactly what a six-volt automobile battery weighed in those days, but it was damned heavy. When we got back to the place on the river where I had followed the alien's tracks, Bush lit up the ground with the portable spotlight. It was much better than a flashlight, but we still couldn't track the alien beyond the grass at the river's edge.

Bush called out the names of a few people that he knew who lived across the river on the Mexican side, but he got no response. We went back to Presidio; there was nothing more we could do that night.

It was past midnight by the time we got back to town, and Cal Darst was no doubt sound asleep. Bush convinced me that it would be better to write a memorandum report and take the matter up with the station senior the following day. That seemed reasonable to me, and I went home and to bed. In my sleep, such as it was, I hunted for that alien and those handcuffs all night.

The following morning, I was at the station with my written report in hand when Cal Darst came in at seven o'clock. He read my memo and said, "Boy, you've got some trouble. Those handcuffs are *capitalized* government property." That was the first time that I'd heard that term. Basically it meant that if it was *capitalized* government property, you couldn't buy it, you couldn't sell it, and you damned well better not lose it.

Cal Darst said that he was going to sector headquarters in Marfa later in the day, and he would give my memo to the chief. George Harrison was Chief Patrol Inspector in Marfa at the time. I'd met him, and he'd given me reason to believe that he liked me. I was pretty sure that he'd stop liking me as soon as he read that memo.

About eight o'clock, Roger Bushner came in and told the station senior that he had a plan to get my handcuffs back. I'd liked Bush from the first time I'd met him, but about now I was beginning to love the man. Cal Darst told him to go ahead with his plan, but he had to deliver my memo to the chief, nevertheless.

Bush and I went back to the spot where I'd lost the alien's tracks the night before. It looked the same in the daylight, and we concluded that the alien could have gone nowhere but into the river. Bush wanted to make contact with someone on the Mexican side, but we couldn't attract any attention from anyone over there. Finally, we moved to some mud flats about three-quarters of a mile farther down river. Bush hollered across a few times, and pretty soon a man on a *burro* came down to the water's edge on the Mexican side.

Roger Bushner knew the border and the people who lived there like few other men. He figured that the man I'd handcuffed was most likely from a little Mexican village called Sierra de Guadalupe a short distance south of the river. He also figured that the man, whoever he was, was probably getting very tired of being handcuffed, especially wrist to ankle. He made a deal with the man on the *burro*: "You go to Sierra de Guadalupe on your *burro*," Bush instructed. "You find the man with handcuffs on his wrist and ankle. You bring him back to the river. We will throw the handcuff key across the river so that you can remove the handcuffs. Then you throw the handcuffs and the key back across the river to us, and I'll throw a twenty-dollar bill across to you. Fair enough?" The man readily agreed, and he immediately left the river to go to Sierra de Guadalupe. Bush and I settled down on the mud flat to wait for him to return. We expected that the trip would take him two or three hours.

Bush's plan seemed pretty simple and could work; although, twenty-dollar bills were hard to come by in those days, and I wondered if the Mexican wouldn't have been just as eager to do it for ten.

Nevertheless, it would be twenty bucks well spent if it got the handcuffs back and saved my job.

We'd been resting on the mud flat for about fifteen minutes when Bush suddenly sat upright. "That Mexican didn't go to Sierra Guadalupe," he said. "He's sitting over there behind that little knoll smoking; I can smell his Mexican tobacco smoke." Sure enough, after Bush brought it to my attention, I could smell the pungent odor of cheap Mexican tobacco smoke, too. It was looking like our Mexican friend was trying to put one over on us.

After about thirty minutes, the man came back to the river leading his *burro*. The *burro* had obviously been sleeping; he was barely awake, and they hadn't had time to get to Sierra de Guadalupe and back. The man immediately started to spin us a yarn: "There are three men missing from the village. I'm not sure which of them is the handcuffed man yet……."

Bush stopped him in the middle of the first lie; "We know that you didn't go anywhere! You've been sittin' over there smokin'. You've lost your chance to make some easy money, and someday you're gonna pay for tryin' to cheat us." The man lowered his head, took his *burro* by the reins, and disappeared back the way he had come.

On the way back to Presidio, I felt like a condemned man. I was mentally packing my bags.

We had only been in the station a few minutes when Cal Darst returned from Marfa with a pair of replacement handcuffs for me….instead of a letter terminating my employment. I can't describe the relief that I felt.

I, of course, had to take a certain amount of ribbing from the other officers in the station, but my assignments didn't change, and it began to look as though I was going to survive, after all. After a week or so the whole matter was forgotten, or at least, I thought it was.

Adequate housing was scarce in Presidio in the early fifties. My wife and I considered ourselves lucky to have gotten a place in *Chotaville* – that, of course, wasn't the official name of the community, but since there was no one living there but Anglo Border Patrol officers, the name seemed appropriate.

Chotaville consisted of ten two-bedroom prefab houses that had started out life on an Army post. Sometime after the war, the Army had no further use for them, so they were disassembled by a group of Border Patrol officers, moved to Presidio, and reassembled on leased land. Each house came with a sixteen-foot Quonset Hut out back and a carport. Another advantage to *Chotaville* was that we had our own well and good water; the city water in Presidio tasted like it had gasoline in it. We were able to rent all of this luxury for eighteen dollars and seventy-five cents a month, utilities included. It seemed like a helluva deal to us. It *was* a helluva deal, even in 1951. We lived in house number two, next door to Cal Darst and his family.

One morning in early January, I was sitting at our kitchen table having an extra cup of coffee with my wife when I noticed a bob-tail cattle truck coming down the street. To see such a vehicle in *Chotaville* was unusual, and it brought to mind a dream I'd had a couple nights before. In my dream, a Mexican man in a cattle truck just like the one that was passing our house returned my handcuffs to me. I remember that he had them dangling from the rear-view mirror. I started to tell my wife about the dream, but before I was able to finish the story, there was a knock on our back door.

When I opened the door, Cal Darst was standing there smiling and dangling a pair of handcuffs over his head. "The man you handcuffed just delivered them to my house," he said. "That was him in the cattle truck. He *is* one of my informants, and he wants to apologize to you for running off with your handcuffs. He was afraid that he wouldn't be able to convince you that he worked for me, so he made his way to the river and called to a friend who lives on the other side. His friend rode across the river on a mule, and then the two of them rode the mule back across the river into Mexico."

One shackle appeared to have been cut with a file and then bent out of shape to slip off the ankle. The other shackle wasn't damaged at all; I have no idea how he managed to get it off without damaging it. I tried my key, and it still worked in both shackles, but the one side didn't appear to me to be repairable. "Looks like they're ruined," I said.

"Ah, they don't look so bad," Cal replied. "We'll take them over to Juan Ochoa's blacksmith shop, and if he'll let us use his forge, I think I can fix 'em."

Cal Darst was an accomplished gunsmith, and he could do wonders with metal, but I still had serious doubts that the handcuffs were repairable.

I pumped the forge bellows while Cal performed his magic. He heated and aligned the two ends of the cut and twisted shackle, and then he said, "Now we'll weld it." I was looking for an acetylene torch and welding rods, but he had no need for them. He stuck the shackle back into the forge until the two opposing ends were glowing red, and then he held them in alignment on the anvil and smacked them several times with a hammer. "That's a blacksmith weld," he said. Then he buffed and polished the metal until the repair was barely visible. They worked perfectly.

I told Cal about my dream, and he looked truly amazed. I'm not sure he believed me, but I swear it's true.

I wrote a memo to the Chief Patrol Inspector explaining more or less how my handcuffs had been recovered. Of course, I didn't mention my dream. I returned the replacement pair that had been issued to me to sector headquarters and resumed carrying my originals. I carried them for years.

Each time that I changed duty stations over the years I managed to hang on to my old handcuffs and take them with me. I still had them in the middle seventies when the government property management regulations changed and handcuffs were no longer considered *capitalized* property. By that time I was District Director in Denver, Colorado, and I had no real need for handcuffs, but I simply didn't want to give them up. Robert McLatcher was the regional property management and procurement officer, and he was a friend. When I told Bob the story behind the handcuffs, he arranged for me to buy them from the government. I paid seven dollars and fifty cents for them; the transaction probably cost more than that in paperwork and bother, but the government set the price, not me. I still have those handcuffs today. Every time I look at them, I recall that incident in Presidio, and it brings back memories of good days and good friends.

Later that year, Jay was involved in a minor incident involving the discharge of his weapon. I don't remember the details, but I heard that he probably would have received a mild reprimand from the chief had he admitted what happened straight away, but he lied, and he was fired a second time. There would be no third chance.

I finished probation in Presidio, and I was transferred to Big Spring, Texas. I'd been in the Border Patrol exactly a year and one week when I was transferred for the third time. I didn't complain, though; I'd made the cut; I'd been promoted and my title was changed to Patrol Inspector – without the belittling *(Tr.)* tacked on.

Roger Bushner had also been promoted and transferred. He was now station senior in Big Spring, Texas. It was the spring that was big, not the Border Patrol station; Lee Butler, Charlie Henderson, and I were Bushner's only troops, but we all got along well, and it was good duty.

The story that I'm thinking of occurred in 1953, about a year or so after I arrived in Big Spring. It taught me an important lesson about people and the risks of law enforcement, and I remember it as though it happened yesterday.

It was a warm Saturday afternoon; Lee Butler and I were working in Lamesa, a small farming town about forty miles north of Big Spring. We weren't in uniform, but we weren't exactly *undercover*. The sedan that we were driving didn't have Border Patrol decals on the doors or red lights mounted on its roof, but it didn't need them to be recognized as a law enforcement vehicle at first glance. It had a six foot whip antenna mounted on the rear bumper for one of the old AM radios that the Border Patrol had acquired cheap after the New York City police had worn them out and a sixteen inch *stinger* antenna protruding from the center of the roof for a newer FM police-frequency radio, which may have been the first such radio installed in a Border Patrol vehicle in Texas. We could have removed the AM antenna, but we couldn't get the mounting bracket off the bumper, and there wasn't anything we could do about the stinger on the roof. Anyway, you get the idea; we were in plain clothes, but almost everybody in Texas would have recognized us at first glance and known not only who we were but exactly what we were doing in Lamesa, *almost* everybody, that is.

Just before dark we were sitting in the car on the side of the road when we spotted a short, scrawny, little man who looked very much like an alien walking toward us. He couldn't help but see the car, but he didn't seem to be paying any attention to us. As he came closer, Lee called out to him in Spanish, "Hey! Where you going, *amigo*?"

He came up to the car cautiously and said, "*Buenas tardes,*" with a broad smile on his face. We could see that he was a little suspicious and ready to run, but he hadn't made us for *La Migra*, at least not yet. I kept my hand on the door handle, ready to give chase, just in case.

Lee started feeding him a line, telling him how we were cotton farmers from Amarillo looking for hands to work our cotton fields. We'd heard that there were cotton workers to be found around Lamesa, and we didn't care if they were *wetbacks*. In fact, we'd rather have illegals; they were good workers. I'd chip in with a comment or two from time to time, and our little friend seemed to be enjoying the conversation.

He grinned and laughed at everything we said,

as though it was all a big joke, and then he asked how many workers we needed. Lee told him that we could use twenty or so. He said that our car wouldn't hold that many, laughing and grinning all the while. By this time, Lee and I were grinning and giggling along with him. He was a pleasant little guy, and we were enjoying the banter.

Still grinning, he said that he could get us all the cotton choppers we wanted, but we'd have to get a truck to haul them. Then he asked how much we would pay him. Lee told him that we wouldn't pay anything for the workers, but we would make sure that he got the best job on the farm for helping us round up a crew. I jumped in and told him that he could be the *mayordomo* and run the whole crew. That seemed to excite him, and the more excited he got, the more he grinned and giggled.

We parted company that evening after arranging to meet him in a roadside park near the migrant labor camp about sundown the following day. He promised to have twenty cotton choppers for us, and we promised to have a truck big enough to haul them to our farm in Amarillo. As he walked away, he looked back over his shoulder, grinning and laughing, and he waved to us. Lee and I waved back, grinning and giggling like a couple of high school girls.

On the way back to Big Spring, we discussed how to best carry out this operation. We decided to use Lee's 1947 Studebaker pickup truck for transportation – I don't recall if we discussed how we would get twenty aliens into a half-ton Studebaker pickup truck, but we didn't have access to anything bigger. Anyway, our first job was to sell the idea to Roger Bushner; without his okay, we were going nowhere.

Lee Butler – God bless him; he should have been a used car salesman – explained the whole thing to Bush, except for the grinning and giggling part; he didn't mention anything about that. Bush *bought-in* immediately, and he *allowed as to how* it was a great idea.

We met at the Border Patrol station Sunday afternoon and worked out the rest of the details. We figured that our little friend was not familiar with the area, or he would have recognized our Border Patrol vehicle the previous day. And it was not likely that any of the aliens that he brought to us would be any more familiar with the area than he. So Bush decided that Lee and I would go to the park in Lee's pickup truck, load the aliens into the back, and have our little friend ride in the front seat between us. Then we would drive around Lamesa making several quick turns to confuse their sense of direction before heading south toward Big Spring, instead of north toward Amarillo.

He would be waiting in a marked car at another roadside park along the highway. When he saw us go by, he would give chase and stop us with his red-light – it wasn't actually a red-light; it was a red plastic lens fitted over the car's spotlight and held in place by wire springs, but it served the purpose. Bush would then question everybody and determine that the Mexicans were *wets* and that Lee and I were transporting them illegally. He'd arrest everyone and order us to follow him to the jail in the truck. It seemed to us like a good plan. Lee and I jumped into Lee's pickup and headed for Lamesa.

We found our *mayordomo* standing beside the highway near the migrant labor camp. He didn't recognize us in the pickup truck until we pulled up next to him and spoke to him. Then he started grinning and laughing as he had the day before, and, of course, Lee and I had to turn on the smiles, too.

He admired our new vehicle but noted that it might be just a little small for our purpose. Lee told him that our big truck had a flat tire, and this was the best we could do. He was also unhappy that the back of the truck didn't have a cover; the *wets* would have to ride out in the open where they might be seen by *La Migra*. We convinced him that this was all we had, and it was this truck or nothing. The *wets* would have to crowd together in the back and take their chances of being seen, but since he was the *mayordomo*, we'd let him ride up front with us. That clinched it; he grinned, giggled a bit, and nodded his approval. Then he let out a sharp whistle, and people started coming out of the bushes all around us. I made a quick count; there were nineteen men, twenty including our *mayordomo*, just as he'd promised. I wondered at the time what he would have come up with had we ask for a hundred.

We loaded the men into the back of the truck; it was a tight squeeze, but we got them all in. The poor little pickup was way overloaded and looked as though it was squatting on its haunches. Lee pulled away slowly – I think he might have been a little concerned about his pickup at that point, but he didn't say anything. We made a few circles in Lamesa before heading down the road to Big Spring. Our passengers didn't seem to notice that we were heading south.

We had only gone a short distance when our *mayordomo* suddenly straightened up in the seat and said, "Wait a minute! This is not the way to Amarillo!"

Lee never missed a beat; he told him that he had to go collect some money from an ol' boy who lived a few miles down the road. He went on with the story, probably more than was really necessary, about how this guy had owed him money for a long time and never would send it to him. Since we were in the neighborhood, he'd called and talked to him on the telephone earlier in the day, and the ol' boy had told him to come by this evening and he'd have the money for him. That seemed to satisfy our little friend, and he said, "*Andale!* Always, get the money first!" and he laughed and grinned some more.

Suddenly, it struck us both at the same time; our little friend was talking to us in English. We hadn't known that he could speak English, and we both began to wonder if we'd said anything to each other in English in his presence that might have compromised us. Apparently not, because he went on chattering in English, grinning, laughing, and he began telling us his life story. It was interesting to listen to him as he chattered on and on. Among other things, we learned that this wouldn't be his first time to be arrested, and he had on several occasions falsely claimed to be a United States citizen.

When we passed the roadside park, both Lee and I saw Bushner parked well off the highway, but I don't think our little *mayordomo* or any of the *wets* saw him. Our friend was too busy grinning, giggling, and telling us of his many exploits to notice much of anything going on around him. Bush pulled out onto the highway, came up behind us, and put the red-light on us.

As soon as the red-light came on, Butler said, "Damn! It's the Highway Patrol." For the benefit of our friend, I asked Lee if he had been speeding, and he said, "No. I'm way below the limit, but they're stopping us for something. Probably, it's nothing serious, though."

The little man in the middle said, "Probably just give you a ticket and let us go, huh?"

Lee and I said, "Yeah!" in unison. We wanted all of them to think it was the Highway Patrol. We didn't want the *wets* in back to jump out of the truck and scatter when we stopped, which they might have done had they realized that Bush was the Border Patrol.

As soon as the pickup came to a stop, Lee and I both jumped out, ready to grab any of the *wets* who tried to jump and run, but none of them did. They may have been packed in too tight for a quick exit.

Bush played his part well. He talked to everyone in the back and determined that they were all illegal aliens, and then he turned his attention to the three of us in the front. He questioned Lee and then me; we both told him that we were U.S. citizens, of course. He then turned his attention to the little man in the middle, who to our surprise immediately confessed that he was an illegal alien. He probably realized that if he claimed United States citizenship, he would have been charged with transporting illegal aliens.

When he finished questioning everyone, Bush ordered us to follow him to town, and he gave us a stern warning not to get out of the truck until he told us to. We dutifully followed the marked patrol car, each of us lamenting our bad luck, falling into the hands of *La Migra*.

Lee and I were both armed, of course, but our little friend didn't know it. I had my pistol in the waistband of my trousers, under my shirt, but Lee had put his in the glove compartment of the pickup. As luck would have it, we hit a bump in the road and the glove compartment door fell open. The light inside the box came on, and there was Lee's pistol in plain sight. Our little friend made a grab for it, but I blocked his reach and slammed the glove compartment door shut. "Let me have the gun!" he said. "Let me have it! I'll kill him! Then we can still go on to Amarillo."

Both Lee and I shouted, "No!" at the same time.

"It would be stupid to do a thing like that," I told him. "They'll catch us, and then there'll be hell to pay. We'll all three of us go to prison, or maybe get the death penalty."

He didn't give up easy, and he continued to argue that we should let him kill the officer. "If I knew we had a gun, I'd have killed him back there where we stopped, and we wouldn't be in this fix," he declared.

I noticed that for the first time since we'd met, he wasn't grinning and laughing. All of a sudden our jovial little friend had turned grim. He was seriously proposing the murder of a federal officer. He didn't seem to be such a nice, friendly, little guy, anymore. The relaxed atmosphere that had prevailed in the cab of the pickup truck was no more. Both Lee and I were tense from then on, and there was no more friendly conversation.

When we were inside the county jail's fenced compound, Bush marched the nineteen aliens into the jail first. Lee and I stayed outside with our former friend while he booked the aliens. When he came back outside, Lee and I pleaded with him to let us go; we didn't know anything about transporting illegal aliens. We'd encountered these guys on the road where their truck had broken down, and we were just giving them a ride to town. Our *mayordomo* was only too happy to back up our story. Bush gave us a stern warning and told us to get out of there. Then he took the last alien into the jail.

A short while later, we called the jailer and told him about the jovial little guy who was the last to be booked, and we suggested that he might want to keep a close eye on him.

Cal Darst, Roger Bushner, Lee Butler, Ray Morris, Darrell Warren, and the rest remained among my closest friends for many years. Robert St. Clair retired long ago, and I believe he's living in McAllen, Texas, now. The others are gone; they and so many of my other friends from over the years have passed away. I miss them all, and I miss the old days. I went on to higher level positions in my career with the Immigration and Naturalization Service, and I suppose that I had more prestigious titles over the years, but I can't help but notice that when retirees get together, the talk always goes back to our early days in the Border Patrol. *Patrol Inspector*, it was the best job we ever had.

\+ + + + + + +

Those were the days!

by

Ed Woods

In the fall of 1963, I was a sector pilot in Marfa, Texas. We would occasionally pull details up into the *nawth country*, as Texans called it in those days, looking for *gottaways*.

G.W. Archer was an Assistant Chief Patrol Inspector in Marfa at that time, and he would often lead the details. I liked working with G.W.; he knew the area well, and he was a master at keeping several P.I.s in line and covering a lot of ground efficiently.

G.W. was a gentleman, but he had a habit that grated against my soul; he continually chewed a wad of tobacco and at the same time puffed on one of his stinkin' *Lovera* cigars. And in the airplane he carried with him a cut down quart milk container full of dirt to spit his tobacco juice into.

Now, I've put up with a lot of nonsense from P.I.s and aliens in Border Patrol airplanes over the years, but a cat box full of dirt and tobacco juice spilled all over inside the cabin is not one of the things that I was about to put up with. "G.W.," I told him, "If you spill a drop of that mess, you're gonna be cleanin' it up yourself. He allowed as to how he was an assistant chief, and maybe he'd decided who would clean it up. I replied that I was the *pilot*, and I was in charge in the airplane.

We took off early in the morning for a look-see at the fields out around Leveland, Texas. G.W., of course, had a fresh wad of tobacco in one cheek and was merrily puffing away on a cigar sticking out the other side of his mouth. He had his little box of dirt clamped in one fist between his knees. He looked ridiculous and smelled worse.

We had no more than gotten off the ground when the wind came up suddenly, as it is prone to do in that country, and blowing dust cut our visibility down substantially. I spotted a fairly large group of people working in a field up ahead of us, but with the blowing dust, I couldn't get a good look at them. I wanted to see just what *breed of cats* they were before I called in the troops on the ground.

I came in low through the dust over the field. Almost too late, I saw the power lines directly in my path. I gave the engine full throttle, lots of back stick, and I made a steep left turn away from the power lines. It undoubtedly saved our lives, but it was kind of a wild ride, especially for someone who wasn't expecting it.

When we leveled out, I looked back over my shoulder at G.W. He looked a little green, and his eyeballs were rolled back into his head. "Are you all right, G.W.?" I hollered over the engine noise.

"You smart-ass! You made me swaller my cud of tobaccah!" he replied.

"I just saved your life! Is that the thanks I get?"

His reply isn't fit to repeat here, but I suppose

that you can imagine the blue words that bounced off the back of my head for the next five minutes.

I finally found a flat road, landed, and let the poor feller vent in all four directions. After a while, he settled down and we took off and worked the rest of the day without further incident.

The people working in the field that I first spotted turned out to be legal, but before the day was done we rounded-up a bunch of wets.

You know, the amazing thing is: G.W. never spilled a drop from that cat box, not on that flight or any of the many others that he made with me after that day. I don't know how he managed it.

I often find myself chuckling at memories of incidents like this from thirty or forty years ago. What a job! Ahh, those were the days!

\+ + + + + + +

Arizona Justice

by

Gerald A. (Jerry) Dahlberg

Blythe, California, was a small back-up station in the fall of 1952. George Charboneau was the station Senior Patrol Inspector, and Marion Taylor, Jim Grasswick, Ed McGee, and I made up the rest of the station force. We checked the farms in the area from time to time in the daytime, but most of our work was at night on the two roads leading from the border to U.S. Highway 60, which was the main highway between Phoenix and Los Angeles in those days.

The Ogilvie Trail was a direct route from California's Imperial Valley to Blythe on the west side of the Colorado River, and U.S. Highway 95 was a straight shot from the border to Quartszite, Arizona, on the eastern side. They were both secondary roads; the U.S. highway was paved, but the Ogilvie Trail was just a gravel road. Neither was heavily traveled, but they were both well-maintained year around.

It wasn't unusual for an enterprising soul living in one of the border towns with an automobile and a touch of larceny in his heart to try to supplement his income by hauling a carload of a*lambristas* north. Of course, they were violating the federal laws by transporting illegal aliens, but if we caught them in Arizona the closest federal court was in Phoenix, and on the California side the federal court was in Los Angeles. We sure couldn't drop everything and rush off to Phoenix or Los Angeles every time we caught a transporter with a half-dozen illegal aliens, but we didn't want to just let the drivers go after we caught them breaking the law. That would have encouraged others, and before long everyone in the valley with an automobile would have been hauling illegal aliens to Blythe. We found an alternative deterrent in the state law, and it worked pretty well.

To transport people, including illegal aliens, for hire required a taxi license. If you didn't have the taxi license and were caught transporting passengers who had paid for the privilege, you were violating the state law, and you could be prosecuted in the state courts. Instead of calling them alien smugglers or transporters, we called them *Wildcat Taxi Operators*, and we hauled them in to the local Justice of the Peace. The fines didn't amount to much, but they usually took the profit out of the illegal enterprise and discouraged the practice somewhat.

One Sunday evening, I believe it was in October, Cal Darst and I were working together on the Arizona side of the river. The Blythe station was in the El Centro Sector at that time, and Cal was the Assistant Chief – Ed Parker was the Sector Chief at that time. Cal had come up to Blythe earlier in the day on an inspection trip, and he decided to work with me that evening.

Shortly after dark we were about ten miles south of Quartzsite on Highway 95 when we encountered an obviously overloaded, rickety, old four-door sedan headed north. We wheeled around in the road and chased the car down. The driver knew who we were, of course, and he didn't want to stop, but he had no choice. He didn't have a prayer of outrunning us in that old car, especially with the load he was carrying. As soon as we pulled up behind him and flashed our headlights, he pulled over to the side of the road and stopped.

Sure enough, he had seven illegal aliens crammed into a vehicle designed for a maximum of five including the driver. He had picked them up south of Yuma and was taking them to Blythe to catch the Greyhound bus to Los Angeles.

Each of the aliens admitted crossing the line illegally and to have paid the driver ten dollars for the trip to Blythe. The driver didn't have a taxi license. I don't recall that we ever caught an illegal alien transporter who did have a taxi license. Of course, alien smugglers as a group have never been a particularly bright bunch of people.

We searched the aliens and put them into the back of our Chevrolet panel truck, and then proceeded to Quartzsite, where we would charge our *taxi driver* with operating a wildcat taxi in violation of the Arizona statutes. We let him drive his own car and follow us to the Justice Court. It was just a misdemeanor charge, and he wasn't likely to run. Even if he did try to get away, we wouldn't have had any trouble catching him in that beat up old car.

In 1952 Quartzsite wasn't anything like it is today. There were no RV parks, fast food restaurants, truck stop service stations, outdoor markets, or curio shops. Matter of fact, there wasn't much to speak of there at all. A gas station with a small automobile repair shop and a café stood on the north side of the road at the junction of Highway 60 and Highway 95. A short distance away there were about ten one-room cabins available for rent to weary travelers, and scattered around in no particular order in the surrounding desert north of Highway 60 there were twenty or thirty private homes, most of them well-used trailers and unpainted shacks constructed of salvaged building materials. The two highways were the only paved streets, and there were no stop signs or traffic lights anywhere in town.

After ten o'clock at night, for all practical purposes, the town of Quartzsite was closed. The only light that could generally be seen after midnight was the glow of a naked bulb hanging from a pole over the gasoline pumps and the orange glow of a dim light left on at night inside the café to discourage burglars.

Originally the town had been known as Tyson's Well, and it owed its existence to an underground river that provided an abundant source of fresh water in the arid desert. It had been a crossroads community, a place to rest and a source of fresh water, since the first prospectors began working their placer claims in the area about 1862. After the Civil War, when settlers began to transit Central Arizona on their way to a new life in California and disappointed forty-niners began moving in the opposite direction to try their luck in Arizona, Tyson's Well became an important stop on the trail. The name was changed to Quartzsite when a post office was established there in 1893. Most of the buildings in town looked as though they had been there since that time.

Arizona justice had been dispensed in Quartzsite by Judge Hagley, a duly elected Justice of the Peace, for as long as anyone living there at the time could remember. He was in his fifties when I knew him, and he was sort of a combination of Marryin' Sam and Judge Roy Bean, but he got the job done. He didn't stand for any nonsense or disrespect of any kind, and justice moved swiftly in Judge Hagley's court.

Judge Hagley's courtroom was small. It had at one time been a bedroom in his home. He had converted it to a courtroom when he was elected Justice of the Peace. There was barely room for his crudely constructed bench, his wooden chair, and a shelf for his law books. Defendants, law enforcement officers, witnesses, and spectators all stood throughout the proceedings; there was nowhere to sit.

When we arrived at Judge Hagley's court just before midnight, we had to stand in line. There was a deputy sheriff with a scruffy looking kid he had arrested for burglary, a highway patrolman with an out-of-state speeder in tow, and a couple of love-struck kids from California who had come across the state line for a quickie marriage all waiting for the judge to make his appearance. He had retired for the night, but the deputy sheriff had aroused him and he was expected momentarily.

After we waited about ten minutes, Judge Hagley came in and took his place behind the bench. He was dressed in pajamas and an old woolen bathrobe, which he had left open down the front just enough to allow us all to see the single action Colt revolver he carried under a belt about his waist. He banged his gavel on the desktop as a signal to us all that court was in session.

The judge quickly disposed of the first cases. He bound the young burglar over for trial and set his bail at $100. He fined the speeder $20, which he collected on the spot. He didn't offer a receipt and the man didn't ask for one. Then he married the California couple in two minutes flat, collected his $10 fee, and turned his attention to us.

I started to explain the case, but the judge cut me off in mid-sentence. He asked our wildcat taxi driver, "How do you plead?" Our man said, "Guilty." And he really sounded guilty, the way he responded in a low voice with his head down and his eyes half closed. The judge banged his gavel, fined our man the $60 the aliens had paid him, banged his gavel again and said, "Court's adjourned! Goodnight everybody!" He got up and walked out of the room, leaving the rest of us standing there. We had barely cleared the room and were standing on the porch when the lights went out. The whole thing had taken less than fifteen minutes.

Our taxi driver got back in his car and headed back down Highway 95 toward his home in Yuma. He probably grumbled all the way home about the goddamn Border Patrol and the unfairness of it all.

Cal Darst and I headed for Blythe to process our illegal aliens and arrange for their transportation back to Mexico. As we were crossing the Colorado River, Cal turned to me and said, "Jerry, are you sure the judge didn't marry me to that highway patrolman?"

\+ \+ \+ \+ \+ \+ \+

Snakes Alive
by
Bob McCord

It was about 1959 or 1960, I suppose. I was a fresh young patrol inspector stationed in Kingsville, Texas. My partner, Richard Dunagan, and I were returning to the station after several hours checking traffic on highway 77, a rather desolate stretch of highway in those days. Rick was driving and I was riding shotgun in the right hand seat. We had been checking traffic all day and had no apprehensions for our trouble. I'll admit that I was a little tired and bored when I spotted a rattlesnake coiled on the edge of the road. I pulled out my trusty Colt New Service .38 Special and casually took a shot at the critter. Much to my surprise, and wonder of wonders, I was pretty sure that I'd hit him.

Rick pulled the car off the side of the road and stopped, and I walked back to collect my trophy. I started to put my foot on the snake's head, intending to grab him by the tail and cut off his rattles to add to my growing collection. There was one little problem with my planning, though; that damn snake wasn't dead! I'd missed him, and he was objecting seriously to what I had in mind. He coiled himself tightly, ready to strike, and his rattles were singing that familiar song that we all dreaded to hear. And there I was, frozen! I was standing on one foot with the other hiked in the air ready to stomp, but Mr. Rattler was having none of that.

Exercising perhaps the quickest move of my life, I jumped up and back at the same time, barely managing to get out of the snake's range. We, that is, Mr. Rattler and I, decided then and there to call it a draw. He uncoiled and slithered away into the brush. I stood there for a minute or two and watched him go, all the while taking deep breaths to get my pulse rate down before I blew a gasket.

That part of Texas surrounding the King Ranch is infested with rattlesnakes; I believe that there might be more snakes per acre there than anywhere else in the world. Although I don't recall many incidents of people actually being bitten by a rattler, they're nevertheless dangerous, and they were everywhere. Everyone in the county was always on the lookout and careful not to step in the wrong place at the wrong time.

Snake hunting became a part of most of our patrols in those days. We held that it was a public service, so to speak, maybe saving someone a nasty bite. Wets were not as common in those days as they are today, and thinning out the rattlesnakes broke up the monotony of a long patrol and didn't detract much from our Border Patrol duties.

A few weeks after my stand-off with Mr. Rattler, I was working with Herb Vinson cutting sign on the King Ranch in a jeep. Ranch hands had cleared fire roads all around the ranch to protect the ranch property from brush fires, and these fire roads, cleared of all brush and grass, made excellent drag roads for our purpose.

Herb was driving slowly, and I was hanging out the right door looking for footprints in the soft, sandy roadbed. The warm weather and the monotony of watching the jeep's wheels go 'round and 'round was beginning to lull me to sleep. My eyes were getting droopy, and every now and then I'd have to stretch my neck and shake my head to break the trance. I was about half dozing when we passed a pile of Mesquite brush on the side of the road and I found myself face to face with the biggest Western Diamondback that I'd ever seen. I woke-up in a hurry! I pulled that big, heavy Colt New Service revolver in near record time, and my shot didn't miss that time. Mr. Diamondback lay dead in the road.

Before we went on with our sign cutting, we hung that dead snake over the barbwire fence so that the ranch hands could see it, admire its size, and perhaps appreciate what we had done to protect them. Its tail touched the ground on one side of the fence and its head on the other. That's how big that son-of-a-gun was, must have been close to seven feet long.

Percy Mosley, an old-timer in the station, mentioned to me one day that I was burning up a lot of ammunition shooting snakes, and he suggested that I just run over them with the jeep when I could. The old-timers would move the jeep slowly and try to catch the snake under the left rear tire; then they would rev the engine and grind the snake into the roadbed. It sounded reasonable to me, and one day when I was driving a jeep back to the station from sector headquarters, I decided to give it a try. It worked pretty well; I got seven snakes in that one short trip. They were all little fellows, about three feet long, crossing the pavement from east to west, but I added significantly to my collection of rattles.

\+ + + + + + +

Standoff at the Salton Sea

by

Bill Botts

I'd been in the Border Patrol a scratch over two years in October of 1988. I'd gotten through the Border Patrol Academy and finished probation without a great deal of difficulty, and I was a journeyman patrol agent.

In my two years of working the line in El Centro sector, I'd caught a lot of aliens and a few smugglers, and I'd even been involved in a few dope cases. I was full of confidence by then; I figured that I'd seen about everything and I could handle about anything that came along. You know the feeling; we all went through it. We'd been around long enough to get comfortable in the job, but not yet long enough to realize just how *serious* this job could get on occasion.

My partner was Tom Younghusband. Tom is a field operations supervisor now, but he was a probationer just short of taking his ten month exam at the time.

Tom and I were working the four to midnight shift, and it had been a quiet afternoon. We were parked off the road near the intersection of California state highway 22 and U.S. highway 86 observing traffic, what little of it there was to be observed. Our job was to back-up the traffic check south of us on highway 86 and check any traffic that might be coming up highway 22. Smugglers were known to use highway 22 in an effort to get around our traffic check on highway 86, and any traffic on that road at night was probably going to be dirty. But there wasn't any traffic.

We'd exhausted about every topic of conversation, and boredom was beginning to set in, when about quarter to eight we received the radio call from sector headquarters advising that an Imperial County sheriff's deputy had been fired upon in the vicinity of Salton City by a white male driving a white over tan 1980 Chevrolet station wagon. The suspect had fled the scene, and we were advised to be on the lookout for the described vehicle.

Tom and I moved father north on highway 86 to South Marina Drive in Salton City to try to intercept the suspect and limit his avenues of escape if he was fleeing south. From that location we could also continue to cover any traffic trying to evade our traffic check point on highway 86.

A few minutes later, sector headquarters call again and told us to meet a sheriff's deputy a short distance away, where he had located the suspect's vehicle abandoned off the side of the road.

When we arrived, Deputy Al Reyes told us that he had stopped the suspect's vehicle for a minor traffic violation, but as soon as he got out of his car the suspect began shooting at him with a handgun. When Reyes took cover behind his vehicle, the suspect sped away. Neither Reyes nor his partner, Deputy Greg Dinsmoor, was hit, but there were three neat bullet holes in the windshield of their patrol car. They had since learned that a suspect believed to be traveling in that vehicle was wanted in San Diego County for murder.

The suspect obviously wasn't familiar with the Salton Sea area. After fleeing from Reyes and Dinsmoor, in a misguided effort to evade them, he had driven off the pavement and tried to drive cross-country in the old station wagon. That effort met with predictable results; the vehicle was stuck in the sand a short distance from the highway.

While we were talking to Reyes, he received a radio call advising him of a report of a prowler at a mobile home on Sea Raider Avenue, which was just a short distance away from where the station wagon had been abandoned. There was a good possibility that the *prowler* might be the individual who had shot at Reyes and Dinsmoor, and the four of us immediately went rushing to that address.

Patrol agents John Parum and Walter "Gino" Harris arrived at the Sea Raider address right behind us; they had been working the traffic check on highway 86 and were sent by the supervisor to back us up.

While the sheriff's deputies talked to the people in the mobile home, we four patrol agents began cutting for sign in the surrounding yard. Tom and I went one way around the house and Parnum and Harris the other way, but it was a useless effort; there were hundreds of tracks going in every direction in the sandy soil.

Directly behind the mobile home there was an old house trailer that looked as though it was abandoned and hadn't moved in years. It was an old model house trailer with two doors on the left side, one at each end, and no other doors. Summoning up all of the tactical training that we could remember, we surrounded the trailer, and I worked my way up to the door near the north end. I pulled the door open from the side, and after assuring myself that the other agents had the open door covered, I took a *quick peek* through the lower portion of the door -- a pair of old ratty tennis shoes that looked as though they were occupied pointing toward the door. Then I went up about half way in the door and took another *quick peek*, shining my flashlight inside. I saw the suspect reclining on a bed with a pistol pointed directly at ***ME***. It was the biggest pistol I'd ever seen, a .44 Magnum. I moved away from the door quickly, I mean *really* quickly, and for some reason that I still can't explain, I threw my flashlight into the trailer. Great! Now I didn't have a flashlight, but that wasn't my biggest concern at that moment. I suddenly realized that this was *real*. This wasn't a training exercise. That guy was going to shoot me if he had half a chance. I wasn't quite so confident as I'd been earlier in the evening.

I shouted as loud as I could, "Throw the gun out and come out with your hands in the air! The trailer is surrounded."

The suspect answered feebly, "I only want to see my kids." Then there was silence.

John Parnum then attempted to open a dialog with him, but the suspect wouldn't answer.

Shortly after we located the suspect, Deputy Jessie Lopez and Undersheriff Ted Whittmer arrived on the scene, and Whittmer took charge. Border Patrol Supervisors John Searle and Don Hoberg also arrived about this time, and the patrol agents secured the area while the sheriff's officers tried to get the suspect under control.

Ted Whittmer finally was able to open a dialog with the suspect, and after about an hour and a half of coaxing and feeding him cigarettes, he managed to get him outside. Whittmer was trying to reason with him, but the suspect was just babbling, completely incoherent, and all of the time he was holding the pistol upside-down to his head with his little finger on the trigger. Finally, Whittmer offered him a last cigarette, and while the suspect was trying to light it, Ted jumped him. They were struggling for control of the pistol when it went off, probably accidentally. The bullet barely missed Whittmer's neck -- he still has stippling of the flesh on his neck from the powder burn.

After almost shooting Ted Whittmer, the suspect managed to break away from him and get back into the trailer with the gun. We were back to step one.

When Ted realized how close he'd come to *buying the farm*, he decided that it was time to bring this drama to an end. He told one of the deputies to bring up the teargas, and he shouted at the suspect, "Alright! We're done f...... around! You throw that gun out here and come out with you hands up, right now!" It wasn't the most prudent statement he could have made under the circumstances; by this time the television cameras were there, and they were pointed directly at him.

A deputy sheriff crawled up to the door on hands and knees and threw a teargas grenade threw the open doorway. Unfortunately, the grenade hit something inside, bounced back out through the doorway, and exploded under the crouching deputy. He was out of the game from then on, and he was still vomiting at midnight when we left the scene. Another deputy approached the door with a grenade launcher and launched a teargas grenade through the open door. The grenade went through the trailer and out through the aluminum skin on the other side. It can probably be found on the bottom of the Salton Sea. Whitmer was grumbling something about needing more training with teargas when we heard the single shot from inside the trailer.

After waiting a reasonable period of time and not being able to get any response from the suspect inside, two deputies cautiously went in. The suspect was dead; he had shot himself in the chest.

I went inside the trailer to retrieve my flashlight, and I saw the body stretched out on the floor. He was a tall, skinny guy, filthy, dressed in tattered clothes, and his arms and upper torso were covered with tattoos. Ted Whittmer later told me that he was a *speed freak* from Fallbrook who had an extensive criminal record. When San Diego County sheriff's deputies were searching his apartment in Fallbrook for narcotics, they found a dismembered body in the freezer. Apparently, that's why he was running.

Oh, yeah, I almost forgot; about that gun; it wasn't really a .44 Magnum. It was a single action .22 caliber with an 8 inch barrel, a cheap knock-off of a Colt *Buntline Special.* It sure fooled me; when I was looking straight into the business end, it looked like a cannon.

\+ \+ \+ \+ \+ \+ \+

Gerry Tisdale,
the scouts and the dogs
by
Brenda Tisdale

My husband, Gerry Tisdale, entered the Border Patrol as a Patrol Agent (trainee) at Laredo, Texas, in June of 1970. Shortly after he graduated from the Border Patrol Academy, the kids and I joined him in Laredo.

The kids were getting to the age at that time where they were becoming interested in scouting. Busy as he was with his Border Patrol duties, Gerry always found time for the kids, and he got into scouting along with them. He was first a Cub Scout leader, and then, as the kids moved along in scouting, Gerry moved up the ranks with them. He was a Scoutmaster, then District Camping Chairman, and by 1984 he had worked his way up to Chairman of the Aztec District of the Boy Scouts of America. He was also by then a Supervisory Border Patrol Agent at the Laredo South station.

Jose Garza was Chief Patrol Agent in Laredo in 1984, and one day he approached Gerry about possibly setting up some sort of scouting program for local boys and girls sponsored by the Border Patrol. Gerry suggested an Explorer program based on federal law enforcement. Chief Garza thought that was a good idea, and he asked Gerry to begin setting it up.

Several months later, Explorer Post 1924 of the Boy Scouts of America, sponsored by the Laredo South station of the United States Border Patrol, was born. Gerry was appointed the first Post Advisor, and Roberto Molina, Michael O'Barr, and Mary Blevins were made assistant post advisors.

Shortly after receiving the post charter, an open house was scheduled to recruit members into the new Explorer post. The first members were a mixed group of ten boys and girls.

A Border Patrol Explorer uniform was designed by the members and the advisors that identified the members with the Border Patrol but was enough different from the agent's uniform to exclude any possibility that the Explorer Scouts would be mistaken for agents. Gerry designed a unique shoulder patch based on the design of the original, Department of Labor, Border Patrol badge of 1924.

With the help of Chief Garza, Gerry and the other advisors planned a program of training and activities that included basic law enforcement training, ride-alongs with agents on routine patrols, community service projects, and funds raising efforts.

The Border Patrol Explorer program became so popular among local teenagers that within three years there were Explorer posts being sponsored by four other stations in the Laredo Sector.

In 1987, Gerry received the Laredo Sector Employee of the Year award, largely in recognition of his work in founding the Explorer scouts program in the sector, and in February of 1988, he was awarded the Boy Scout's Silver Beaver award for having taken the Explorer program to the Border Patrol.

Hugh Brien, then Chief of the Border Patrol, happened to be visiting the Laredo Sector on Washington's Birthday in 1988, and he took in the local celebration and the parade. The Border Patrol Explorers had a float in the parade on which several members rode. Other Border Patrol Explorers in uniform served as ushers in the VIP seating area during the festivities. Chief Brien seemed to be very impressed with the Border Patrol Explorers, and after the parade, he visited with a number of them.

In June of that year, Gerry was summoned to Washington, D.C. Chief Brien had been so impressed with the Laredo Sector Explorer program that he wanted to extend it into other sectors nationwide. Gerry stayed in Washington until October of that year and developed the nationwide program from the ground up. He designed a uniform, a badge, and a shoulder patch to be used nationwide, all based on the uniform and the shoulder patch used in the Laredo program. He wrote the manual for Border Patrol Explorers, setting out specific qualifications and standards for membership, training and development programs, and activities programs, all of which were based on the program as it was in the Laredo Sector.

The Border Patrol Explorer program became hugely successful all over the country, and Gerry was awarded the Immigration and Naturalization Service Commissioner's Special Award for his outstanding contribution to the program.

About that time, the Border Patrol decided to bring dogs back to enforcement operations. The Border Patrol had previously used dogs in the fifties, but they hadn't worked out very well at that time. The dogs had been obtained from the Air Force, and they had been trained as guard dogs. Neither the dogs nor their handlers were well-trained for Border Patrol law enforcement work, and the dog program was discontinued in 1958 following a few unfortunate incidents. This time around, the Border Patrol was determined to do it right.

Gerry was selected as the first dog training instructor, and he was sent on detail to the national K-9 school in Tuscalusa, Alabama, for training. After he completed his training, he traveled for the next two years from sector to sector, wherever the Border Patrol had dogs and their handlers to be trained and certified. As the Border Patrol acquired more and more dogs, it became apparent that this system wasn't going to work, and Gerry was detailed to El Paso, Texas, to begin setting up a Border Patrol K-9 training academy.

On January 2, 1992, the National Canine Facility was officially opened in El Paso, with Gerry Tisdale as its first Director. He was promoted to the rank of Assistant Chief Patrol Agent. In the years since, hundreds of dogs and dog handlers have been trained at the K-9 Academy for service in the Border Patrol as well as in fire departments and other law enforcement agencies throughout the Southwest. They even trained some dogs and handlers for Mexican police forces and fire departments.

Gerry retired from government service as Director of the K-9 academy in March of 1995, but he would not enjoy a long and happy retirement. His health was failing, and after an extend illness, he passed away on November 19, 2003. Dozens of Border Patrol officers, active and retired, and more than a hundred law enforcement officers from many different departments in Texas and New Mexico attended his memorial service. Many of the officers were accompanied by dogs that had been trained at the K-9 academy. It was a great tribute to a loved and respected man, and it was a beautiful service.

Gerry and I were married for more than thirty years, and I was privileged to share much of the Border Patrol experience with him. He was the most honest and dedicated man that I have ever known, and I miss him.

+ + + + + + +

Army Surplus

by

Robert J. (Bob) Carney

It was 1992, and I was a Border Patrol Agent in the Imperial Beach station in the San Diego Sector. We were using night vision scopes on linewatch then that the Army had given to the Border Patrol when the military no longer had any use for them. They worked for our purpose better than binoculars alone, but not much better. They had originally been designed to work with the military TOW missile system, and for our purpose they had some serious faults. To begin with they were heavy, and they had a monocular sight that required the operator to keep one eye pressed against the eyepiece all the time that the device was in use. The image was an orange/red color and the resolution was a low range sixty lines. Soldiers fondly referred to this sight as the *Red Eye* for obvious reasons. It also had a loud cooling motor, which added to the discomfort of the operator. Using this scope for any extended length of time usually resulted in a severe headache.

In my other life, before the Border Patrol, I was commissioned officer on active duty in the United

States Army for ten years, and I'd had considerable experience with night vision devices on army tanks and other equipment. I knew that there was better equipment available, but the Border Patrol simply didn't have the necessary funding to be able to provide it to the officers in the field.

At that time, I was also serving as a tank company commander in the California Army National Guard. In one of the National Guard publications I read an article about the Army disposing of its inventory of obsolete M60A3 tanks; some of them were being used as static targets on gunnery ranges, some were donated for display in front of V.F.W. posts and government office buildings, and some of them were being dumped at sea off the coast of Florida to serve as artificial reefs.

I was quite familiar with the M60A3 tank and its weapons systems, having used them over a number of years while on active duty in the Army. I knew that the M60A3 tanks were fitted with the Tank Thermal Sight, commonly referred to as the TTS, and I knew that these devices would have to be removed before the Army disposed of the tanks. What I didn't know was what the Army planned to do with all of the Tank Thermal Sights after they were removed from the tanks.

The Tank Thermal Sight had a number of advantages over the old TOW missile scope: The TTS had 120 lines of resolution, twice that of the TOW missile scope, which would provide a much better image, and it had a much greater range than the TOW missile scope. The TTS also projected the image on a six inch screen instead of through a monocular eyepiece, which would allow a single agent to scan for targets for much longer periods of time. Of course, the TTS would have to be mounted in a vehicle; it couldn't be used as a hand-held like the TOW missile scope, but that small burden could be overcome. The advantages of the TTS far outweighed the inconvenience of having to mount it in a vehicle. It would be ideal for Border Patrol linewatch operations. Perhaps the Army could be persuaded to part with a few of them. It wouldn't hurt to ask.

I made a few telephone calls and discovered that all of the Tank Thermal Sights were being sent to Anniston Army Depot in Alabama. Some of the sights were sold along with some of the tanks to foreign governments, but the depot had lots of surplus sights on hand. Fine! How do I get them? I was referred to the Armaments, Chemicals, and Munitions Command in Rock Island, Illinois.

Before I went any further with this idea, I wrote a memo to Bill Pink, the Patrol Agent-in-Charge in Imperial Beach, setting out all of the reasons why I thought we should attempt to get some of the surplus Tank Thermal Sights for use in our linewatch operations. Mr. Pink thought that it was good idea, and he and I convinced Chief Patrol Agent Johnny Williams that the Tank Thermal Sight would be superior to the TOW missile scope in clarity, range, and dependability.

A demonstration of the Tank Thermal Sight was arranged for a Border Patrol representative, George Van Horn, at Fort Huachuca, Arizona, and he confirmed everything that I had said about it to Border Patrol Headquarters. I was given the green-light to go ahead trying to get them from the Army, with the codicil, however, that there would be very little Border Patrol money available for this project.

I called the Armaments, Chemicals, and Munitions Command in Rock Island, Illinois, where I spoke to the Weapons Systems Manager, Mr. William E. Boles, a civilian employee of the Army. Mr. Boles turned out to be a bold and patriotic American. After I explained who I was and why I wanted the Tank Thermal Sights, he said that he would do everything that he could to help me get them. He made good on his word every step of the way.

With the considerable help of Mr. Boles at the Armaments, Chemicals, and Munitions Command, I was able to get a commitment from the Army to *loan* the Border Patrol a total of one hundred twenty-eight Tank Thermal Sights. Unfortunately, they were in Fort Bragg, North Carolina, and Anniston, Alabama, and the Border Patrol didn't have the money to pay for their shipment to San Diego or anywhere else. It was time for some good ol' fashioned Border Patrol ingenuity: I called the Air National Guard.

I found an Air National Guard unit in New York that had a C-130 coming to Southern California. I explained my predicament to the commanding officer, and he agreed to stop in North Carolina, pick up our Thermal Tank Sights, and deliver them to the Naval Air Station North Island in Coronado, California.

The Army at Fort Bragg was kind enough to remove them from the tanks, pack them for shipping, and deliver them to the flight-line at Pope Air Force Base. They even loaded them onto the aircraft. When they arrived at NASNI in California, the Navy flight-line crew helped us get the boxes off the airplane and load them onto Border Patrol trucks. It was a good day for the Border Patrol; we had half of our night scopes, and it hadn't cost the Border Patrol a cent.

Now, how do we get the rest of them from Anniston, Alabama? What the hell, I called the Air

National Guard again. The Air Guard unit at Channel Islands, California, had a C-130 available and they were willing to help, but it wouldn't be so simple this time. The sights were out of the tanks, but they had to be individually packed for air shipment and loaded onto the aircraft, and the Army couldn't do it for us in Alabama.

The California Army National Guard had a nine man counter-drug team under the command of Sergeant First Class Dan Cooke, known as Team Shadow, working with the Border Patrol in the San Diego Sector. These soldiers immediately recognized the potential benefit of having access to the Tank Thermal Sights for borderline surveillance, and they volunteered as a group to go with me to Alabama over a weekend and help pack and load the sights onto the aircraft. And I pressed my wife into service; she was also a Patrol Agent at Imperial Beach.

There were eleven of us in the party, and we arrived in Anniston, Alabama, on Saturday. We had brought the sixty-four packing crates that the sights from North Carolina had been packed in with us, and by Sunday afternoon we had the Anniston sights packed and ready to go. When the airplane returned from completing its other missions that weekend, we loaded-up and we were on our way back to California.

The Tank Thermal Sights, as the name implies, had been designed to be mounted in army tanks, and they weren't going to fit in Border Patrol vehicles without some ingenuity and a bit of re-engineering. The sights were, as I mentioned, only on loan to the Border Patrol, they still belonged to the Army, and I didn't dare make any unauthorized alterations to them. I was going to have to build a platform to mount the sights in such a way that they would serve our purpose in linewatch operations without tampering with the sight itself.

Bill Pink, who was by this time an Assistant Chief Patrol Agent at sector headquarters, realized what I was up against, and he detailed a veteran sector mechanic, Lenny Lulow, to help me. Lenny is an amazingly resourceful individual, and together we built the first prototype of the Mobile Thermal Scope.

The prototype was installed in a Chevrolet Blazer, which also came to us compliments of the U.S. Army via the California Air National Guard at no cost to the Border Patrol. It worked perfectly. Chief Williams was so proud of our accomplishment that he frequently had me demonstrate our Mobile Thermal Scope to VIP visitors. We were all proud of it.

I continued to manage the program from the old Imperial Beach Border Patrol station for the next two years, and we acquired twelve more vehicles from the Army and turned them into Mobile Thermal Scopes. Each of these additional vehicles was delivered to the Border Patrol by the Air National Guard as a courtesy. Ultimately, eight of the scopes were put to work in the San Diego Sector, four in the El Centro Sector, and one was sent to Guam.

Mounting the scopes on the platforms and installing them in the vehicles was accomplished with the help of Chenowith Racing Products of El Cajon, California, at a cost of about $25,000 for the whole project. High Intensity Drug Trafficking (HIDTA) funds were used for this purpose. There was very little other expense to the Border Patrol, and we had thirteen viable and effective night vision scopes. By comparison, one of our Inframetrics night vision scopes now in use costs $65,000, and that's without the vehicle.

This project was certainly a bonus for the Border Patrol, but the most gratifying part for me personally was to see how everyone involved from the beginning to the end, Mr. Boles, Sergeant Cooke and the soldiers of the regular Army and the Army National Guard, the airmen of the Air Force and the Air National Guard, the sailors at the Naval Air Station North Island, the folks at Chenowith Racing Products, and everyone else who took a hand so willingly and without reservation when they understood what we were doing and the importance of the Border Patrol mission to protect our borders. Some of these folks had never before given the Border Patrol a thought, but they jumped in with both feet to help us in every way that they could.

Border Patrol funding has been increased dramatically in recent years, and today's Patrol Agents use state-of-the-art electronic surveillance equipment. We no longer use the Mobile Thermal Scopes, and the Tank Thermal Sights have all been returned to the Army. They are not rusting away in some government warehouse, though. They are now being used once again in army tanks by a unit known as the *Opposing Force* at the Army's National Training Center at Fort Irwin, near Barstow, California.

\+ \+ \+ \+ \+ \+ \+

A Very Mobile Organization

by

Roger P. (Buck) Brandemuehl

I entered the Border Patrol on August 1, 1956, at Yuma, Arizona. I was living in Greeley, Colorado, when I got *the call*, and I didn't want to leave my wife and daughter alone while I was at the academy. So I pulled our magnificent twenty-eight-and-a-half-foot house trailer to Tucson, Arizona. I had a sister living there who would be company and help for my wife while I was away. I figured that we could pull the trailer on down to Yuma after I finished at the academy, but it didn't quite work out that way.

While I was at the academy, I was told that I had been transferred to El Paso, Texas. So in my time off I started looking around for a place in El Paso to live in our trailer; I planned on hauling it to El Paso after I graduated.

The day I graduated from the academy I was told that I had been transferred again, this time to Lordsburg, New Mexico. Of course, like all recruits, I had been told that the Border Patrol was a *mobile* organization, but I never expected it to be *that* mobile: I had less than six months service, and I'd already been transferred twice.

I went back to Tucson, hooked the trailer onto the car, and the Brandemuehl family was off to our new home in the delightful but thrifty Tumbleweed Trailer Court in Lordsburg, New Mexico. It was the only trailer park offering water, sewer, and electric hook-ups in Lordsburg at the time, and the Tumbleweed lived up to its name in every way.

Our little house trailer came with only the basic necessities, so I invested in a small black and white television set. After erecting a forty-foot antenna, we managed to get a snowy picture on two or three channels, which was about all that anyone got on television in Lordsburg at that time. We didn't have a lot, but I had a steady job, and we were happy. Actually, we were hoping that my tenure in Lordsburg would be longer than it had been in Yuma and El Paso and we wouldn't have to pull-up stakes and move again for a while.

For the benefit of those of you who are unfamiliar with the Southwest, Lordsburg is located about half way between El Paso and Tucson on Interstate 10. Of course, the freeway wasn't there in 1956; it was U.S. Highway 80, a narrow and busy two-lane strip of pavement with a sixty mile an hour daylight speed limit and a fifty mile an hour speed limit after dark. It was considered to be a long trip to either El Paso or to Tucson then, and none of us went to either place very often.

Lordsburg in those days was a lot smaller than it is today, and it looked pretty desolate to a newcomer. It was quite a shock to some of our wives when they arrived, but they soon settled-in and acclimated, as

Border Patrol wives tend to do wherever they find themselves.

Living may have been a little primitive, but the work was great in Lordsburg. We had a full range of activity, freight trains, traffic checks, farms and ranches, sign-cutting, even a little *city patrol* from time to time; although, to call Lordsburg a city in those days may be stretching reality a bit.

T.K. Hull was the Lordsburg station senior, and Joe Rufft, Bob Rumbough, Loren Sorenson, C.B. Ramage, Ernie Powell, Norris Tummons, Ned Kent, and I were his troops. Clarence Mathis, Kermit McKnight, Don Clegg, Alan Eliason, and Gene Wickersham transferred in while I was there. They were all good people to work with, and we all got along well.

Depending on available manpower, two to four officers at a time were assigned to physically check each freight train passing through Lordsburg. It was a daunting task considering that some of the trains consisted of a hundred cars or more, box cars, cattle cars, gondola cars, automobile carriers, and the old style refrigerated cars with the ice boxes on each end. Some cars were loaded and sealed, others were empty and the doors open, and you never knew who or what you might find inside.

It's almost unbelievable the places that illegal aliens will hide on freight trains, and they will go to great lengths to conceal themselves. They will get in amongst the animals in cattle cars; they will cover themselves with straw, cardboard, or anything else that they find in open boxcars; they will crawl inside huge rolls of wire or concrete and steel pipes being transported in gondolas or on flat-cars, and we often found them in the ice boxes on the ends of the refrigerated cars.

Crawling over freight trains looking for illegal aliens, sometimes with the train on the move, was dirty, dangerous, and physically demanding work. I sometimes have nightmares that I'm still checking freight trains in Lordsburg.

When I first arrived in Lordsburg, District Director Marcus T. Neeley required us to search freight trains in dress uniform for some reason known only to him. We weren't making a lot of money in those days and most of us only had one dress uniform. And the wool dress uniforms of that era had to be dry-cleaned. Thankfully, that ridiculous policy was changed shortly after I arrived, and we thereafter searched freight trains in rough duty uniforms.

Equipment was very limited in the Border Patrol in 1956, and we often didn't have enough vehicles to go around. I remember checking freight trains one night in Lordsburg when we only had one car for the four of us. A hundred-car drag pulled into the yards and stopped. Our driver dropped me and my partner off at the end of the train, and he and his partner went on to the middle of the train where they parked the car. My partner and I, one on each side of the train, started working toward the middle, and the other team started in the middle and worked toward the front of the train. The plan was for us to work the train until we reached the vehicle and then drive the car to the front of the train and pick up the other team.

About the time that we reached the middle of the train, I thought that I saw some movement between the train and the cattle pens along the north side of the tracks up ahead of us, but I wasn't sure. I told my partner, and we decided that he would take the car and pick up the other guys and I would stay near the cattle pens to make sure that no one got back on the train before they returned. I didn't think that there was more than one man, maybe two, hiding near the pens, and I wasn't worried.

A few minutes later the car pulled up with the lights off, and suddenly the cattle in the pens came to life. They were milling around in all directions, bawling, and making a hell of a commotion. Over the backs of the animals - they were mostly calves - a dozen or more men could be seen climbing over the cross fences in the pens. Obviously, they were illegal aliens who had been hiding among the animals in the pens, and now they were trying desperately to get away from us. Within a minute or so, each of us had at least a couple of struggling Mexicans in tow.

I had an alien in each hand struggling to get them to the outer fence where I could handcuff them so they couldn't get away while I searched for others. As we went along, I kept yelling at them in my limited Spanish: "*Andele! Andele!*" One of them was hollering something to me, but in all of the pandemonium and with my *un-tuned* Spanish ear, I couldn't understand what he was saying. I finally got them to the fence, secured them, and then jumped back into rodeo in the pens. Later, when we had all of the aliens rounded-up, I discovered what my guy had been trying to tell me: He had lost one of his *zapatos* in the chase, and I was making him run over the cinders along the tracks barefoot. It hurt, and he was protesting. I went back and found his shoe for him, but the poor guy limped around the rest of the night.

We all picked up some bumps and bruises chasing the aliens in the cattle pens that night, but that wasn't our biggest concern at the moment. It was the middle of the night, and there we were, four officers, a dozen illegal aliens in custody, and one car. It took several trips to transport all of us back to the station, but we got it done, and we had all of the aliens processed before daylight.

Refrigerated cars on the railroads of that time had ice boxes on each end of the car. These were open spaces the full width and height of the car and about six feet wide intended to accommodate large blocks of ice to keep whatever perishables that were stowed in the middle of the car cool during transit. Each ice box had two heavy hinged trap doors in the roof of the car, which were closed when the car was loaded but intentionally left open when the car was empty to air-out and dry-out the car.

The ice boxes in the refrigerated cars were favorite hiding places for aliens, and we had to climb on top of the train, walk carefully along the catwalk, and check every one of the ice boxes. At night you had to use a flashlight to see in the box, but you didn't want to turn on the flashlight on top of the train; illegal aliens ahead of you would see you coming and be out of the box and on the run before you could get to them. So you would hold the light down inside the box before you turned it on and turn it off again before you pulled your arm out of the box. Yes, it was dangerous and perhaps a bit foolhardy, but that's the way we did it.

One night I was checking the reefer cars on the rear end of a train alone. There were only two of us assigned to trains that night, and my partner had gone ahead to check the cars on the front of the train. I was up on top trying to navigate the catwalk when I saw two men climb out of the ice box of a car a couple of cars ahead of me. I took off trotting along the catwalk after them. I misjudged my leap from one car to the next, and I fell between the cars. I caught my chin on the edge of the catwalk, and I landed on one knee on the coupling between the cars. Then I tumbled off the coupling onto the rail bed and rolled out from between the wheels. Thank God the train wasn't moving! I wouldn't be here telling this story today if the train had been moving. I was stunned, and I just sat there on the edge of the tracks with blood from my chin dripping on my shirt and blood from my knee running down my leg.

I don't know how long I sat in the cinders on the edge of the tracks in a stupor before one of the train's crewmen found me. He shined his lantern in my face and said, "My God! man, you're hurt!" I wanted to come back with something smart like, "Yeah! What was your first clue?" but I just didn't have it in me. A few minutes later, my partner found me. He bundled me into the patrol car, and we went to the hospital.

Doctor Baxter was an old country doctor who treated almost every kind of animal that moved. He looked me over, and he decided that since there were no broken bones, at least none that were protruding through the skin, a few stitches would do, and he patched me up and sent me home. He didn't have a real steady hand, and his stitching hurt damn near as much as the fall.

The following day I was pretty stiff and sore from my fall, but I was able to hobble back to work. I was still on probation, and I was afraid that I'd be fired if I didn't show up for work.

Local law enforcement in Lordsburg was limited to say the very least in 1956, and the Border Patrol was often called upon by the police and the county sheriff for assistance or back-up. If someone called the emergency number about a significant violation of law or emergency in the middle of the night, the chief of police was usually *out* and the county sheriff, who must have been the cleanest man in New Mexico, was always *in the bathtub*; the Border Patrol was invariably asked to handle the situation.

One evening the emergency services operator got a call about a domestic disturbance in the city. The chief of police was *not available*, and the sheriff was apparently taking another bath. My partner and I were patrolling around town waiting for the next freight train to pull in, and we were asked to look into the disturbance. We started toward the location, but before we got there, we were told to disregard the call, so we went back to the vicinity of the railroad and forgot about it.

The next day we discovered what the *domestic disturbance* had been all about. It seems that the chief of police had a girlfriend in town, and he had been visiting his girlfriend the previous evening. The chief also had a pet goose, and the pet goose had followed the chief to the girlfriend's house. The chief's wife had passed by the girlfriend's house on an errand and saw the goose hanging around the front door. She stopped her car and barged into the girlfriend's house unannounced, and she caught the chief and his girlfriend in a rather compromising situation. The fur started flying, and a neighbor who didn't know who was involved had called the police. We later heard that the chief *cooked his own goose* after that episode.

Traffic check in Lordsburg in those days was nothing like it is today. It usually involved two officers, one car, and a stop sign, and we rarely set-up in the same place for more than a few hours at a time. Of course, you never know what you're going to encounter on the highway, and U.S. Highway 80 was a *major* route across the United States at the time. We often had multiple lookouts from other law enforcement agencies seeking individuals wanted for various crimes.

Joe Rutland was the state trooper assigned to Lordsburg at the time, and he often worked with us on traffic check. Together, we corralled a number of unsavory characters besides illegal aliens, and sometimes we managed to help-out a few folks, too.

It was a couple days before Christmas, and we had our traffic check set-up on U.S. Highway 80. About ten o'clock in the evening a Mexican-American family pulled up in an old, beat-up car that seemed to be loaded down with all of their worldly possessions. The father was driving and mama was sitting in the front seat holding a baby wrapped up in a blanket. Three other small children were wrapped in blankets and shivering in the back seat; the heater in the car had stopped working. They were farm workers on their way to California. The father told us that the baby was sick, and they needed to find a doctor. I looked at the baby; it was very pale and not moving at all.

We terminated the traffic check and escorted the family to the local hospital. Unfortunately, it was too late. The baby had died, probably before they reached our traffic check point.

We took up a collection at the hospital that night for the rest of the family; it amounted to twenty or thirty dollars, I think. Then the medical staff at the hospital made arrangements for them to stay free at one of the local motels that night.

The next morning the Border Patrol families in town showed-up at the motel with donations of food for the family and toys for the kids, which made us all feel a little better. You never know what you might get into on traffic check.

One of the most enjoyable and fascinating of all Border Patrol activities to me personally was sign-cutting, the age-old art of looking for and detecting the *signs* left behind when someone or something has passed through a particular place and then following the *signs* until the person or animal is found.

The art of sign-cutting and tracking probably originated in prehistoric times with cavemen tracking down animals for food. It was widely used in the early days in this country by Indians as well as our pioneers for locating enemies, hunting for food, and tracking outlaws, and it survives today for much the same purposes. The Border Patrol has refined the art over the years, and Border Patrol Agents are recognized nationwide for their expertise and are often called upon to help other agencies in difficult searches.

Almost all law enforcement agencies use sign-cutting and tracking techniques to some extent. When I worked in some of our bigger cities later in my career, I was surprised to see how much big city police rely on simple sign-cutting and tracking techniques to locate people, gather evidence, and solve crimes.

In 1956 in Lordsburg, New Mexico, I liked it mainly because it was such a great game. The exhilaration of the chase and the satisfaction of the catch is fun! Of course, I'm sure that ol' *Juan Fulano* and his buddies didn't always think that it was so much fun.

When I was in Lordsburg, we did most of our sign-cutting and tracking in the Playas Valley between the Alamo Hueco Mountains and the Animas Mountains. It is a vast, remote valley where the coyotes yipped, mountain lions roared, and the deer and the antelope played in those days. It was a remarkably wild and primitive area, and in the fifties it still had all of the marks of the Old West. There were vast ranches with names like *Alamo Hueco*, *Double Adobes*, and *Diamond A*, and many of the ranching families went back generations into pioneer days. Even in the middle of the 20th Century, ranching in that area was a hard life, and the ranchers were tough, resilient, and honest to a fault. They made an impression on me that lasts to this day.

Because of the distances involved, it wasn't practical to run back and forth to Lordsburg every day when we were working in the Playas Valley. We pulled thirty-day camping details periodically, and we kept a small camping trailer on the Heard Ranch to live in while we were there.

I believe that it was sometime in the thirties when an illegal alien murdered Joy Heard's brother at the ranch. The local ranchers and cowboys formed a posse and rode into Mexico after the murderer. No one ever talked about what happened in Mexico, but for many years thereafter there were very few *wetbacks* seen in the Playas Valley. Most of the ranchers still hadn't forgotten the murder, and we got a lot of cooperation from them. Joy and Doak Heard were happy to accommodate us whenever they could.

I had been stationed in Lordsburg about two years when the office got information from a reliable source that a number of illegals had been seen in the Playas Valley, and Kermit McKnight and I were sent on a thirty day detail to see what we could find.

We meticulously went over our Jeep to make sure that we had all of the necessary equipment and that everything worked properly, especially our two-way radio. We loaded on a couple of spare tires - we always used six-ply tires on the jeeps, as standard four-ply tires didn't last long in the rough terrain of Southern New Mexico. And we strapped on extra five gallon cans of gasoline. It's a long way between service stations down in that valley. Then we loaded on all of our food and supplies and tied everything down. When we left Lordsburg, we looked like we were going on an African Safari, or maybe the Hillbillies moving to Beverly Hills.

Those old rag-top Jeeps weren't real fast or powerful, and loaded down as we were, we didn't get to the trailer at the Heard Ranch until late in the afternoon, too late to do any patrolling the first day. We unloaded the jeep and set-up *housekeeping* in the trailer. Then we turned our attention to fixing supper. Kermit McKnight was mighty handy with a skillet and a knife, and I definitely was not. So we decided then and there that he was the cook and I was potato peeler and dishwasher. I thought it was a good arrangement; I wouldn't lose a lot of weight from having to eat my own cooking.

There wasn't anything to do after supper but sit around and look at the scenery, which was beautiful out there in the evening but disappeared soon after the sun went down, so we turned-in early.

The next morning, we got up about four-thirty, dressed, grabbed a quick breakfast, and headed over to the west side of the valley. We wanted to get to the far west side before sun-up so that we could cut for sign into the face of the rising sun, which would make any tracks much easier to see than they would be later in the day or with the sun behind us. As we traveled east cutting for sign, we pulled a drag of old rubber tires along behind us to smooth the ground, erase any old tracks, and give us a smooth clean drag road for the next day's cut.

The sunrises are as beautiful in that country as are the sunsets. As the sun comes up over the Alamo Hueco Mountains it showers the mesquite, the grass, and the sand with a brilliance that's hard to describe in everyday workingman's terms. It was a good way to start the day, but sometimes it was hard to keep your mind on business.

It would take us practically all morning to cut all of the drag roads along the border in the valley, and even then we would miss a lot of ground. Much of the terrain was hard-packed *caliche* and some of it was solid rock; trying to cut for sign across the hard-pack and rocks was a waste of time. The Mexican Army could march across it without leaving a track. We cut along the international border as best we could, but there were too many of the hard-pack areas, and they were too large. A determined alien who knew the country, or one who was lucky, could use the natural terrain to get around us rather easily. So if we didn't run across any tracks on our morning cut, we would spend the afternoons visiting ranches, line camps, and windmills looking for information and evidence of any border jumpers we might have missed.

We usually got back to the trailer at the Heard Ranch about dusk, tired and hungry. We carried canteens of water and a thermos of coffee with us for the day, but we seldom carried anything for lunch. By the time we got back to our camp in the evening, Kermit's meals tasted better than anything they might serve at the Waldorf Astoria.

After the supper dishes were cleaned-up, we turned-in for the night. Morning came around early on those details.

I believe it was the second or third day when we came across four sets of tracks going south across our drag road. That was unusual; why would four people go all the way out there in the wild country to go to Mexico? We studied the tracks for a few minutes and then chased them a few yards both ways from the drag road. It was as we suspected; the aliens had turned around a few yards south of the drag road and walked across backwards to make us think that they were traveling south when they were actually going north. It was an old trick then, and it never worked, but the Mexicans kept trying it. I imagine that they're still doing it today, and they still think that they're going to get away with it.

I stood up in the back of the Jeep to get a better look at the ground in front of us while Kermit drove slowly through the brush and over the rough terrain. I'd guide him by shouting, "A little to the left! A little to the right! Take a hard right then straighten out!"

When we determined which way they were going, we would drive on ahead a quarter of a mile or so and check for footprints across any dry *arroyos* and sandy stretches of ground that we could find. We would try to find a sandy creek bed going east and west that anyone moving north would have to cross. Then we would each walk in a different direction until one of us found the aliens' tracks. The one who found the tracks would fire a shot into the air as a signal to the other, who would then get the Jeep and pick him up. Then we would repeat the process a quarter of a mile or so on ahead.

There was no point in trying to follow the tracks step by step until we caught up to the aliens; we would never catch up to them. They didn't have to go slowly looking for tracks in the sand, as we did, and they could move a lot faster. Besides, as I said, the terrain in that country is such that there are long stretches of hard packed earth and rock where they wouldn't leave tracks.

We were using the tracking technique developed centuries ago and refined by the Border Patrol. It worked! It just took concentration and a lot of patience. That particular day we didn't have a lot of patience, so we radioed El Paso and asked for a Border Patrol airplane.

The Border Patrol used Piper Cubs in those days, and our pilots were exceptional; they had to be! Flying over that rough mountainous terrain, sometimes as low as fifty feet above the ground, looking for footprints on the ground and people hiding under trees and brush while piloting the airplane at the same time was dangerous work. Over the years the Border Patrol has lost a number of pilots from crashes while chasing illegal aliens. Dale Burt and Bill Turner were two of the best. I believe that it was Bill who flew out to help us that day.

Bill spotted our Jeep shortly after he arrived in the area, and then he flew on ahead of us to see if he could spot the people we were after or pick up their tracks from the air. It's remarkable how well you can see tracks on the ground from fifty or a hundred feet in the air.

Often the sound of the aircraft would *drive the aliens to ground*, that is, they would stop and try to hide under a tree, in a vacant line-shack or a barn, or even crawl into a culvert if one was close. Hiding usually did them no good; either the airplane pilot or the ground team would eventually follow their tracks to their hiding place, or we would narrow the search area on the ground to where it didn't take long to find them.

On this occasion, we tracked the aliens to a line-shack about eight or nine miles north of the drag road; the tracks arrived, but none departed. We were sure that the aliens were hiding inside the shack, but when we looked they weren't there. Where could they have gone?

There were hundreds of human footprints and cattle, horse, and feral animal tracks around the shack and the adjacent corral; it would be impossible to pick out the ones that we were interested in. So we would have to make a cut around the area forty or fifty yards out from the shack and try to find the four sets of tracks leaving the area.

Then out of the corner of my eye, I saw a man sitting under a tractor in the back of the corral. We had been so intent on searching the line-shack that neither of us had noticed him before. *"Buenas dias, senor!* I addressed him in Spanish. *Donde estan sus amigos?"* He nodded toward some feed barrels near the corral fence. Sure enough, his buddies were hiding inside the barrels.

From time to time we would encounter cowboys on horseback gathering their cattle or tending their windmills, and they would tell us about fresh tracks that they had seen or strangers walking through the valley that they had encountered in recent days. They knew that we appreciated their help, and they knew that we would help them when we could. Without the help and cooperation of the people who lived and ranched in the valley, it wouldn't have been possible for so few of us to cover so large an area.

I remember once coming across a group of cowboys gathering their stock on the Diamond 'A' ranch. They invited us to eat with them at their round-up camp; it was just like in the movies, chuck wagon an' all. After dinner and before bedtime, we swapped some stories, and we even played a little poker. They were a great bunch of guys, and I felt privileged to share some time with them.

Today the Border Patrol is much larger and far better equipped than we were, and illegal aliens are so numerous that they don't have the time to track down individuals and small groups close to the border as we did. Working the wild country and the long camping details like I have described are probably things of the past in the Border Patrol. It's too bad. It was a good life, and those of us who had the privilege of *working the line* in that era will never forget it.

\+ + + + + + +

You Have the Right to Remain Silent!

by

Bill Chambers

It was about 1952 or 1953, as I recall. Tex Ewing, Buck West, and I were nearing the end of a four-to-midnight shift in Harlingen, Texas, when we decided to check-out a little cafe where we had previously found an illegal alien.

The entrance to the dining room was on a main street, and there was a door leading from the kitchen into an alley that ran along the side of the building. There were no other doors that we knew of. We parked the old green Border Patrol pick-up truck that served as our *patrol car* in those days in the alley and looked through a small window into the cafe's kitchen. Sure enough, there was an alien that we had apprehended there once before working in the kitchen.

Buck West remained behind in the alley covering the back door, and Tex Ewing and I walked around to the front and entered the cafe's dining room. There were no customers at that time of night, and the only one in the dining room was a pleasant young waitress, who might be described as *pleasantly plump*.

Well,...maybe a little more than *pleasantly...* Alright, she was fat! We were in uniform and she knew exactly why we were there, but we identified ourselves, anyway, and told her that we were there to check the kitchen help. She just shrugged her shoulders, and we continued on into the kitchen.

Jose, who we had clearly seen through the window was nowhere in sight. Where could he have gone? We had the only two doors and the windows covered, so we were sure that he was still in the building. There was a storage area above the restrooms. Tex and I grinned at each other; that had to be where he was hiding. We climbed the stairway and searched the storage area, but still no *Jose*. Tex went into the men's room; there was no one there.

I had successfully completed the Border Patrol Training School and recently completed probation. I was confident that with all of this considerable and intensive training behind me, no Mexican illegal alien was going to out smart me. There was only one other place that he could be hiding: the ladies' room! And I went barging through the door, hot on the trail of my quarry... Uh-oh!

Lo and behold, there bigger than life, and I do mean bigger, was a replica of the waitress with her drawers down sitting on the throne. I was at a loss for words. I summoned all of my intensive training, intellect, and experience, and I said,..."You have a right to remain silent!" Then I hurriedly backed away and closed the door.

A few minutes later, we located *Jose* hiding under a stack of wooden Coca Cola boxes. The first words out of his mouth were, "*Yo tengo papeles!*" And he did have immigration papers. He produced an official looking document from his pants pocket and handed it to me. It was a copy of his previous deportation order.

I will always be grateful that the lady in the restroom remained there until after we left the premises.

\+ + + + + + +

The Cripple Was Crooked

by

Dale Musegades

Back in 1987, I was Chief Patrol Agent in El Centro, California. We were seizing a lot of vehicles in those days, and occasionally we'd grab one that had a hidden compartment of one type or another built into it for the explicit purpose of smuggling something, usually people or drugs. It was standard practice to remove these secret compartments before the vehicle was put up for auction, but occasionally one would slip by for one reason or another, that is, removing it would damage the vehicle, removing it would cost more than the vehicle was worth, or somebody just failed to notice that it was there. I suspect that the van that Mr. Lopez – that's not his real name, but we'll call him that for now – bought at the public auction still had the hidden compartment under the floorboards because removing it would have weakened the structural integrity of the vehicle, but that's only my opinion.

Anyway, Mr. Lopez, who was partially paralyzed but seemed to be able to get around fairly well, paid eleven hundred dollars for the van and drove it away. No one expected to hear from him again, but that was not to be.

A few weeks after the sale, Mr. Lopez called my office and complained that upon his return from a short trip to Mexico, his van was surrounded at the port of entry by twenty officers who were all pointing machine guns at him. Of course, we knew that was an exaggeration; there were never that many officers on duty at the port of entry at one time and they didn't generally point machine guns at people during routine inspections, but we listened to his complain, anyway.

He claimed that his van and everything in it was thoroughly searched and he was embarrassed. When the officers found nothing in the van, they told him that the reason he had been searched so thoroughly was because the description of the van was in U.S. Customs computer, apparently due to the drug smuggling activities of the previous owner. He requested that I immediately take the necessary steps to have the lookout on the van removed from the computer. I told him that I didn't have the authority to do that, and I referred him to the U. S. Customs Service. So long as that hidden compartment remained in the van, I didn't think it was a good idea to take the lookout off, and I wouldn't have done it if I had had the authority, but I didn't tell Mr. Lopez.

Mr. Lopez wasn't going to take no for an answer, and he went to his congressman for help. And when the congressman couldn't or wouldn't help him, he decided to take his troubles to the local newspaper.

At that time, a woman named Virginia wrote a daily column called *Probe.* Anyone with an axe to grind about anything could air their grievances through Virginia. As a rule, Virginia had been very fair and objective with the Border Patrol, but for some reason she thought that we were being mean spirited and unfair with this poor crippled man who often *had* to make short trips to Mexico to care for his crippled mother. For a while, it seemed as though everyone in town was supporting poor Mr. Lopez, and I was catching hell from all sides.

After being figuratively beat about the head and shoulders for several days by Virginia and others who had decided to take up the cause of this poor crippled little man being abused by the big powerful Border Patrol, I called Virginia and asked her to have Mr. Lopez bring the van in so that I could look at it and try to resolve the matter one way or another. She agreed, and a few days later Mr. Lopez brought the van to Sector Headquarters.

First, I offered to buy the van back from Mr. Lopez; although, I had no idea how this could be legally accomplished. It didn't make any difference; Mr. Lopez now wanted twenty-five hundred dollars for his eleven hundred dollar purchase. He said that the van at auction was only worth what he had paid for it at the time, but now it would cost him at least twenty-five hundred dollars to replace it. He had a point; most seized vehicles were sold at auction for far less than their real value, but I knew that there was no way that we could take the van back and allow him a fourteen hundred dollar profit. So that option was definitely out of the question.

Next, I offered to trade his van for another seized vehicle of approximately the same value. I didn't know how I would accomplish that, either, as all such vehicles were turned over to the General Services Administration for disposal shortly after seizure, and the Border Patrol no longer had any authority over them. It didn't make any difference. He wasn't interested; he liked the van he had.

I offered to have the hidden compartment removed at government expense on condition that he would sign a letter absolving the government of responsibility should the removal weaken the structural integrity of the van. He refused to sign such a letter. I was at wits end, and then something clicked in my mind; I'd seen Mr. Lopez before.

A few months previously, we had encountered a smuggling ring taking smuggled aliens around our traffic checkpoints on highway 86 and highway 111 by transporting them across the Salton Sea, a large body of brackish water in the middle of the desert some thirty miles north of El Centro. The smugglers had a fourteen foot aluminum boat with an outboard motor. They would put five aliens and a number of gasoline cans in the boat at the south end of the Salton Sea, and then they would motor north until they were past our checkpoints. Then they would pull into shore, offload the aliens into a waiting vehicle, and proceed with them on to their destination. When we caught them, we arrested five aliens and three smugglers, and we seized the boat and two automobiles. Mr. Lopez was one of those arrested that night; he was the leader of the ring.

Then it was clear; Mr. Lopez didn't want another vehicle, and he didn't want the hidden compartment in the van removed. What he wanted was to be waved through the port of entry without being searched, and I wasn't going to let that happen.

I advised Virginia of Mr. Lopez' prior record of smuggling, and to my surprise, she printed it in the *Probe*. I suppose that's about as close to an apology as you can expect from a newspaper. I never heard from Mr. Lopez again.

+ + + + + + +

Giant Jean Ferre
by

Bob Stille

It was a cold Saturday morning when I got a call from an informant who wanted to meet me in a pub in Magog, Quebec, Canada. It wasn't far from Derby Line, Vermont, but the weather was terrible, typical for that time of the year, cold and blustery, near zero temperatures, and a lot of snow on the ground. I bundled up, put on my heavy fur lined boots, my fur cap, and my parka, and I headed out to meet the guy. I'm five inches over six feet tall in my socks, and I think I weighed about two-eighty at that time. Bundled up like I was, I probably looked taller and like I weighed at least four hundred pounds or more.

The pub in Magog was in the basement of a small hotel. It was about ten o'clock in the morning when I got there and walked down the stairs and into the dimly lit barroom. Apparently, French Canadians like to start their drinking early on Saturdays, I thought, as I looked around. The place was really rockin'. It was full of men well on their way to oblivion; the number of empty beer bottles on the tables made their intention pretty clear. I'd estimate that there must have been about fifty well-oiled Canadians reeling around in various stages of inebriation.

Not wanting to be conspicuous, I strolled in, sat down at one of the empty tables, and ordered a beer. I had no more than been served when a couple of the men started talking to me in French. I don't speak French, more than a few common words and phrases that we all picked up working on the Canadian border, and I told them so in English, which for some reason seemed to seriously offend them. Suddenly, one of them pointed at me and hollered, "Giant Jean Ferre!"

I had no idea what the man meant, but it seemed obvious that he was mistaking me for someone else. I tried to explain to him that he was mistaken, but he was having none of it. Several of the others began gathering around, and it was obvious that they were fighting mad about something. I was in the middle of a chorus of drunks chanting "Giant Jean Ferre!" and I didn't know what the hell they were talking about. There was no mistaking, though, that I was about to get a Royal Canadian ass-kickin' if I didn't do something pretty quick. I stood up and backed up against the bar, ready to fight off as many as I could before the lights went out, my lights, that is.

At that point, the bartender, who was my informant, intervened and started shouting at the crowd. Of course, it was all in French, but from what I could gather through all the shouts and curses, he was telling the men that I was not Giant Jean Ferre, whoever in hell Giant Jean Ferre was. It took a while, but he finally convinced them, and they quieted down and went back to their drinking. I started breathing normally again.

A while later, I got an opportunity to talk privately with my informant, the bartender, and I asked him, "Just who is this Giant Jean Ferre?" He explained that Giant Jean Ferre was a professional wrestler who was about seven feet tall and weighed close to four hundred pounds. Giant Jean and some other wrestlers had put on an exhibition match the night before in Sherbrook, Quebec, which is just a few miles up the road from Magog. After the wrestling match, Giant Jean and his buddies went to a popular night spot between Sherbrook and Magog where they all got stinkin' drunk. One of the locals in the place apparently said something that one of the wrestlers took offense to, one word led to another, and pretty soon the brawl was on. Of course, the professional wrestlers led by Giant Jean Ferre made short work of the locals; they threw a bunch of them out into the snow.

It was the losers from the night before who were sitting in the pub in Magog licking their wounds and plotting revenge when I came strolling in completely unaware of what had happened the night before. I guess, bundled up as I was, through their blurry eyes I looked for all the world like the giant wrestler.

\+ + + + + + +

We Must Have Done Something Right!

by

Gene Botts

I came home from the U.S. Navy with no money and no real prospects for a decent job. A friend told me that the Border Patrol was taking applications, and he suggested that I might want to apply. I'd grown up in Central Arizona, and I'd seen Border Patrol officers around from time to time, but I knew next to nothing about what they did or how they went about doing it.

I'd joined the Navy on impulse on my way to work one morning without the slightest idea of what I was getting into, and I thought it might be a good idea to know a little about what I was doing this time. I found a ten-year-old book on the Border Patrol in the library, and I picked up a two page pamphlet at the post office. I sat down and read them both in one evening, and, of course, the old book and the slim pamphlet told me everything that I needed to know. Border Patrol! That's for me! Sign me up!

Over the next couple of months, I took and passed the written test, and I somehow I managed to sneak through the oral interview. Then I heard that they were only going to hire about two hundred trainees from a list of more than a thousand who had passed the written test. I didn't have a spectacular score on the test, and I thought that my chances of being hired were somewhere between zip and squat.

I went on with my so-called life, and I'd almost forgotten about getting into the Border Patrol when, almost a year later, I got a telegram telling me to report to Calexico, California, on October 14, 1957. The Border Patrol was actually going to hire me; I was astonished! Had someone made a mistake? Or had I somehow managed to slip through the cracks?

Calexico was a good six hour drive from Phoenix in those days of narrow two-lane highways, and I arrived late on Sunday afternoon. I knew that I was a day early, but I was excited, and I went directly to the Border Patrol station. A rather gruff and unsmiling Senior Patrol Inspector met me at the door and greeted me with, "What do *you* want?"

I stammered something in reply and showed him my appointment letter.

He looked at the letter briefly, grunted, and said, "Can't you read? It says to report at 8:00 A.M. on the 14th. This is the 13th. What are you doin' here today? Come back in the morning,… and don't be late!"

I hadn't gotten more that a couple feet inside the door, and it was quite obvious that I had been dismissed. I said, "Thank you, sir." I should have left it at that, but as I was turning around to leave, I stopped, and I asked a really dumb question: "Where can I stay tonight?"

He gave me an exasperated look and said, "I think I'd get a room somewhere."

When I got back to the parking lot where I'd left my car, I realized that I'd left my keys in the ignition, and I'd locked the doors. I walked across the street to the city firehouse and borrowed a wire coat hanger. While I was attempting to hook my car keys with the coat hanger through the crack between the glass and the doorframe, the Senior Patrol Inspector came up behind me.

"What are you doing?" he asked.

"Locked my keys in the car," I replied, a bit embarrassed.

He didn't say a word directly to me, but as he walked away shaking his head, I overheard him say, "Oh, for Chris' sake!"

At that moment, I thought that my chances for meaningful, long-term employment in the United States Border Patrol were fading fast.

I found a room in a cheap motel on the edge of town, but I couldn't sleep that night. I'd quit my job in Phoenix to join the Border Patrol, and I thought about driving back to Phoenix that night so that I could be there early Monday morning and beg for my job back before they hired someone else to replace me. I finally settled down and went to sleep; if worse came to worse, I could always go back to the Navy.

The next morning I was feeling a little better. I got dressed and had breakfast at a little café near the Border Patrol station. I lingered over my coffee, watching the time carefully. I was going to report at exactly eight o'clock, not a minute early and not a minute late. I'd gotten off to a bad start the day before, but even a lame squirrel gets a nut now and then.

Maybe that grouchy old son-of-a-bitch wouldn't be there.

Six of us reported to Calexico that morning, and as I'd hoped, there was a different Senior Patrol Inspector on duty. He introduced himself as the station senior, and he wasn't any friendlier than the other one had been the day before. He collected our appointment letters, mumbled something about welcome, and then without another word, he turned us over to another officer. As we left his office, one of the other guys remarked, "He seems about as happy to see us as he would a boil on his butt." I didn't say anything, but I'd come to the same conclusion. This could be a difficult year.

The six of us were crammed into an automobile that had seen better days, and we were taken to El Centro to meet the Chief Patrol Inspector for what we all thought would be our official welcome into the Border Patrol.

The chief was a tall, handsome, deeply tanned, stern looking man with a South Texas accent. He looked us over with a cold, unsmiling expression on his face for what seemed like half an hour but was probably less than a minute before he said a word. When he finally spoke, he went on for at least five minutes non-stop, but there was not one word of welcome. About all that I remember about the chief's *welcome aboard* speech was his final remark just before we left his office: "I'll be surprised if two of you are still here at the end of your probationary year."

After we left the chief's office, I believe it was the same guy who made the remark about the Senior Patrol Inspector in Calexico who wondered out loud but softly, "Is everybody in this outfit a horse's ass?"

Our class wouldn't start at the academy for about a month, so we were put to work riding with a journeyman officer, except for tower duty, which wasn't exactly mentally demanding. There were three towers along the international border fence in Calexico at that time, and during daylight hours an officer manned each tower alone, keeping watch for intruders from the south. It was hot and uncomfortable in the towers and everyone hated tower duty; so the trainees got their fair share early on.

For some reason, I'd taken to smoking cigars. I really don't know why; I didn't enjoy them that much. When I started in the Border Patrol, I was twenty-one years old, but I looked to be every day of sixteen, and I had overheard some snide comments about my looks and my age. Maybe I thought that the cigar made me look older and more mature. I doubt that it did; it probably just made me smell bad.

Anyway, one morning it was my turn in the tower, and I parked the jeep in the shade directly underneath the tower and began climbing the ladder. I had a cigar clinched between my teeth, and about halfway to the top, I noticed that burning embers from the cigar were falling on my shirt, my brand-new, expensive uniform shirt. Without thinking, I spit the cigar over my shoulder and continued climbing to the top. A few minutes later, I happened to glance down at the jeep; there was a fine curl of smoke coming straight up from the center of the canvas top on the jeep. My cigar had landed on the canvas top and set it afire. I'm sure that I broke all known speed records for climbing down a steel ladder, but by the time I got down and put the fire out, there was a perfectly round eight inch hole in the canvas.

I spent the rest of that shift trying to make up a good story to explain that one, but in the end I decided that I had better tell the truth. I got a good chewing-out from my unit supervisor and my first opportunity to write an incident report. I was really worried; trainees could be fired for no reason at all in those days, and I was sure that my days in the Border Patrol were numbered.

I later learned that even the chief laughed when he read my incident report. Everybody was laughing about it, but I looked upon it as just another nail in my coffin, and I was collecting quite a few nails. The other trainees were talking about what they planned to do after they graduated from the academy. After all the stupid things I'd done that first month, I was thinking about what I might do when I got dumped from the academy.

In time I would come to know and respect the supervisors and senior officers who seemed to be so demanding, stern, and unfriendly when I was on probation; they were fine men. It was all an act, part of the testing process, and it served us well for many years. It weeded out those who were just looking for a paycheck.

With only a few exceptions, the 71st session of the Border Patrol Academy consisted of recently discharged military veterans, and Robin Clack, who was the academy chief at the time, wasn't always impressed with our deportment. However, we all *wanted* and *needed* the job, and our time in the military had taught us to pay attention to directions and follow orders. Of course, we complained and whined constantly about the weather, some of our classmates, some of our instructors, the chief, and especially the cooks, but I don't recall anyone ever complaining about the Border Patrol as an institution. It was the best job most of us had ever had; we were proud of it, and we all wanted to become a permanent part of it. As I recall, everyone intended at that time to remain in the Border Patrol for life, ….if we could just get through the next few months without being fired.

Perhaps, it was because of our attitude that our class did a little better than most academy classes in those days. One hundred thirty-four of us started in the 71st. session, and one hundred twenty-eight graduated. I think Chief Clack was shocked that so many of us made the cut; he seemed to be a little disappointed.

Of the six of us who stood in the chief's office in El Centro that day in the fall of 1957 to be welcomed into the Border Patrol, four of us successfully completed the probationary year, and three of us would go on to retire from the Immigration and Naturalization Service more than thirty years later. Several of my classmates became District Directors and Chief Patrol Agents, and many of us reached middle management positions before retirement.

I remained in the Border Patrol until December 1964 when I transferred to Investigations in Chicago. With the exception of a short stint as an Examiner and a two-year tour as an Immigration Officer in the Bahamas, I spent the rest of my career in Investigations, but I've never forgotten the best days of my life in the Border Patrol.

About the time that I retired, my son, Bill, followed me into the Border Patrol; I don't think that he ever seriously considered doing anything else. He's a Border Patrol supervisor in Mississippi now.

Today there are hundreds of other sons and daughters, nieces and nephews, even some grandsons and granddaughters of officers of my era serving in the Border Patrol. That so many of them have chosen to follow in our footsteps is sincerely gratifying. We must have done *something* right!

+ + + + + + +

Memories of Sign-Cutting

by

Wes Selman

I was cuttin' sign along the line
When I spied a track headin' north
The design was mesh, and the track looked fresh
So I followed it for what it was worth

The stride was short and the depression light
And figured it wouldn't be long
Til' I caught sight of a little mite
From way down in Michoacan

But after a while, I guess about a mile
I hadn't caught sight of the dude
His stride was short, but he was makin' me
work
Now that alien was bein' down right rude

The tracks went here, and the tracks went there
You know, they began to meander a bit
He sure wasn't lazy, but I thought he was crazy
When actually, he'd just stopped to sit

Recuerdos

The ground was hard, but now and then
I'd see a twig that was broken or bent
And the sign that he left for me to see
Told me steadily northward he went

The sun had moved high and it brightened the sky
And shone down with oppressive heat
My stomach began to growl and send a complaint
It was tellin' me that it was time to eat

So I found a tree that offered some shade
And that's where I parked my jeep
Then I broke out a burrito of tortillas and beans
And I ravenously began to eat

And as I savored that Mexican delight
With the aroma wafting in the air
I began to feel that I wasn't alone
Because from somewhere I could feel a stare

As I gazed about, I saw a Mesquite
That grew thick and close to the ground
And from out of that bush, I could see two eyes
Starin' at me, big, and round

I called, "*Oiga Jose, ven para ca!*"
"*Tienes hambre y quieres comer?*"
And as he emerged from that thorny bush
He did so with a dignified air

Recuerdos

An extra burrito I had in my pack
And I offered it to Guanajuato Joe
And after he'd eaten and had a drink
I said, "Let's load up, it's time to go!"

Back at the station, I unloaded my catch
With all the paperwork yet to be done
I'd been up since four, and my feet were sore
I'm tellin' ya, I was ready to go home

As I filled out the forms and took his prints
I asked an important question of Jose
"Who do you know, and where were you goin'?"
And he replied, "*Yo tengo parientes en L. A.*"

I finally got home after a long day afield
And mused as beer ran down my chin
Come six o'clock the very next morn
I'll be out there trackin' aliens again

1991

The Nasty Boys

by

Ray Harris

I was patrolling the dairy farm region near Chino, California, one day with a partner who is still in the Border Patrol; so I'll just call him *partner* for now.

As we drove through the dairy reserve, the air was thick with the smell of ammonia and bovine excrement; it was almost as if a vile curtain of stale air separated in front of us as we moved along.

We soon spotted two young gentlemen in an old, beat-up, car who became obviously dismayed by the sight of our marked Border Patrol unit, and they showed their displeasure at our presence by flooring the accelerator of the old car and speeding away.

We made a quick three point turn and gave chase. When we turned on the overhead red lights, we were prepared for whatever they might do; we suspected that they might bail out of the car and take off on foot. And bail they did! Both of them were out and running before the car came to a complete stop. Of course, they were in very good physical condition from the rigors of their every-day jobs on the dairy farm, and they almost jumped the four foot high barbed wire fence in a single leap. Unfortunately, both of them just barely tipped their toes on the top strand of the wire fence, and they both landed face down, magnificent belly-flops, in the muck. Then they slid face down for about four or five feet in some of the nastiest mixture of cow poop, bovine urine, and God only knows what else.

They stood up and looked each other over, not particularly concerned about us for the moment. They were both covered in slime and muck from head to toe; the only white parts visible were their eyes and their teeth.

My partner and I, still on the other side of the fence, cracked up laughing; we were doubled over with laughter, so much so that we couldn't begin to think about climbing the fence and arresting these guys. The Mexicans stood there grinning at each other for a minute, and then they took advantage of our momentary immobility. They took off running in the opposite direction at a good clip. I yelled after them in Spanish to stop, but they didn't even slow down. They had no worry; it was obvious to us, and it must have been obvious to them, that we had no chance of climbing the fence and catching up to them. Besides, neither of us was anxious to go running through that slop in our clean uniforms, ... and we wouldn't have been thrilled to have them in the car with us if we did catch them.

We got back into the car, and as we were leaving, my partner said, "They looked a lot like citizens to me."

"Yeah, U.S. citizens," I replied.

\+ + + + + + +

Was it that long ago?

by

Orville Lewis

I was a young Patrol Inspector, just starting my career in the Border Patrol, and I was working the four to midnight shift in El Paso, Texas. I was in the station squad room for some reason that I can't remember now, when Patrol Inspector Zigler came in with a man that he had caught making an illegal entry from Mexico near the Santa Fe Railroad Yards. This particular individual didn't appear to be Mexican; he was a large man, and his facial features were more European than Latin. Zigler didn't know exactly what nationality he was, but he had seen the man sneak across the border, and that gave him sufficient cause to arrest him and bring him to the station.

Zigler sat him down and was trying to write him up, but he didn't seem to be getting anywhere. All of his attempts to question the man in English and Spanish were met with bewildered looks and blank stares.

Patrol Inspector Scarantino, who spoke Italian, happened to be in the station, and he tried to question the man in Italian. He wasn't getting through to him, either. The man just looked at him and smiled.

One of the other guys had picked up a little German during World War II, and he tried, "*Sprechen die Deutsch*?" There was no indication of recognition from the man, just a blank stare and a faint grin.

About that time, Zigler noticed that the man had a small metal box in his shirt pocket. Attached to the box was a wire and at the end of the wire an earplug. "No wonder we're not getting through to him," Zigler said. "This guy's deaf, and he doesn't have his hearing aid in his ear."

Zigler pushed the earplug into the man's ear and turned the small dial on the box about half way up the graduated scale etched into the metal case. Then they went through the questioning routine again, English, Spanish, Italian, German, with about the same results as the first time. The only apparent difference was that now the man was grinning and nodding his head in a sort of rhythm. Frustrated, Zigler turned the dial on the metal box all the way up to maximum. The man jerked his head up, rolled his eyeballs around, and grimaced.

Zigler decided that the hearing aid must not be working. He pulled the earplug out of the man's ear and stuck it into his own ear. Music! Loud music! Very, very loud Music! He immediately jerked the earplug out of his ear.

That was our introduction to the transistor radio. They had only recently come on the market, and not one of us had seen one before. Was it really that long ago?

\+ + + + + + +

Galveston, Oh Galveston

by

Roger P. (Buck) Brandemuehl

My wife was diagnosed with Leukemia in the fall of 1958. I was stationed in Lordsburg, New Mexico, and the medical facilities there could not provide adequate treatment for her. I took her to a hospital in El Paso, and the doctors there strongly recommended a hospital in Houston, Texas. We, of course, didn't have the resources to commute regularly from Lordsburg to Houston for her treatment, and she couldn't have withstood the long trips in any event. I shall always be grateful that the Service granted my request for transfer so that I could arrange the best possible treatment for my wife.

I arrived in Galveston, Texas, in June of 1959. Don Jordan was in charge, and Hank Henderson, Dan Soloman, Allen (Frito) Fry, Miles Adams, Don Day, Glenn Smith, Cliff Howard, and I were his troops. They were a great bunch of guys to work with.

The Galveston Border Patrol station had been opened primarily as a *crewman control* station only the year before. There had been a steady increase over the years since World War II in the number of foreign crewmen who were deserting their vessels in United States ports and remaining in the country illegally, and the number of stowaways on vessels arriving in United States ports was also on the rise and becoming a major concern to the Service. To meet the challenge, Border Patrol stations were opened in Florida and along the Gulf Coast, and INS investigators were assigned to crewman control duties on the East Coast, the Great lakes seaports, and on the West Coast.

Galveston and its neighboring port, Texas City, were ranked among the top five seaports in the United States for shipping when measured by tons of cargo. We were also responsible for crewman control at the ports of Beaumont and Port Arthur, Texas, which were smaller than Galveston but busy seaports, as well.

Crewman control duties kept us pretty busy, but we were expected to do other, more conventional, Border Patrol duties, such as *city patrol* and transportation checks, as time and manpower permitted.

In Lordsburg I had been almost exclusively exposed to Mexican aliens who had entered the country without inspection, but in Galveston we were seeing aliens from everywhere who had entered the country or tried to enter the country in a variety of different ways and violated sections of the immigration laws that I had never before given a thought. What a change! It was almost like having to learn the job all over again.

Immigration Inspectors John Mulkey and Roland Miller were stationed in Galveston at that time, and both were very competent, excellent officers, easy to get along with and easy to work with. They, of course, inspected the ships upon their arrival, but it was our responsibility to see to it that any crewmen or stowaways that they ordered detained-on-board stayed on the ship and departed from the United States with the ship. We made periodic unannounced and unscheduled visits to the ships all the while that they were in port to verify that the people ordered detained-on-board were *in fact* on board.

There was a fairly heavy fine levied against the ship if an alien ordered detained-on-board got off the ship, so some shipping companies opted to hire security guards to watch over them, which made our job easier. Other companies made little or no effort to prevent these aliens from leaving the ships.

The law requires that the captain of an arriving vessel present any stowaways on board to the inspecting officer at the time of first inspection, but captains don't always know of stowaways on their ships. We frequently had to search ships that we suspected may have had stowaways hiding on board. When I was in Lordsburg, I was often amazed at the ingenuity of Mexican illegal aliens to conceal themselves on freight trains. I soon realized that the Mexicans on the trains in New Mexico were rank amateurs when compared to stowaways on the ships arriving in Galveston.

There are at least a thousand places to hide on a modern seagoing freighter, and the older and dirtier the ship, the more places there are to hide. Searching ships isn't fun; it's time consuming, physically demanding, dirty, and dangerous work, not to mention that stowaways are often the bottom of the socio-economic ladder from some of the dirtiest and most disease-infested and crime-ridden foreign ports in the world, and you never know what they're likely to do when you find them.

Climbing up and down ladders in dark holds, and searching through cargo such as bundled bananas, automobiles and trucks, packages of all kinds, and bulk grain and ore, all of which provide good hiding places for stowaways, is challenging to say the least. And making your way along damp, slick catwalks to search lifeboats in their davits and other closed spaces on the weather decks is dangerous. Hank Henderson found out the hard way a few months before I arrived when he fell into an open cargo hold and was seriously injured.

Sometimes we would have to board and search vessels anchored out in the entrance to the harbor, which seafaring men call *the roads*. The Coast Guard would take us to and from the ship in one of their boats, and we would have to board and leave the ship by means of a *Jacobs Ladder*, a rope ladder with wooden steps, one end secured on deck, and the other end thrown over the side of the ship to the boat in the water below. Climbing a Jacobs Ladder from a small boat to the deck of ship is challenging in fair weather, and darn near impossible in inclement weather and choppy seas, but somehow we did it. I have nothing but praise for the Coast Guard boat coxswains' skill at timing the swells to put us on and take us off the Jacobs Ladders.

Ship's captains are required to report any missing crewmen and aliens ordered detained-on-board to the INS prior to the ships departure. When we would receive such a report, we would go aboard and interview the captain and other crewmembers who might have known the missing individual and know where he might be going in the United States if he intended to desert. We would also get as good a physical description as possible and search his cabin and any personal belongings left behind in an effort to learn where he was going. Then we would begin a local search for him.

Galveston was a wide-open town at that time. There were many *sailors bars* on the waterfront, and prostitution, if not officially condoned, was generally ignored by the local police, all of which proved to be the downfall of many a foreign crewman. Quite often we would find our missing sailor in one of the bars or one of the bawdy houses, or in jail charged with drunk and disorderly conduct or some other minor offense. If we found him before the police got him, he got a quick ride back to the ship before it departed. If he was in jail on a minor charge, he would often be turned over to us for *deportation*, sometimes after paying a small fine.

If we couldn't locate the missing crewman within a reasonable period of time, we would distribute *lookouts* to our contacts at the bus station, in the bars and bawdy houses, to the local police, to taxi drivers, and even to derelicts on the waterfront. We had a system worked out, and we could practically cover the whole town with *lookouts* in a matter of hours. We paid a twenty-five dollar reward for information leading to the location of a deserting crewman, and this small incentive was often enough to have our missing sailor in custody in short order.

A crewman who was determined to desert his vessel and remain in the United States illegally; one who had a well-thought-out plan of action, was a different matter. Such an intentional deserter was not so easy to locate. If we received timely notification, we could, and we often did, locate and arrest the alien before he got out of the area. Galveston is on an island, and there are limited means of transportation to the mainland and away. But a determined alien, especially if he had help from someone, such as a smuggler, a friend, or a relative, could get by us and blend into the East Texas population rather quickly. When that happened, we would try to develop information about where he was going and who he might contact there. We would then send the information on to the Border Patrol or INS office having jurisdiction.

Of course, missing crewmen cases in Port Arthur and Beaumont were more difficult to handle because of the distances involved; it was about seventy-five miles to Port Arthur and about eighty miles to Beaumont. Thankfully, the volume of shipping in Port Arthur and Beaumont was much less than in Galveston and Texas City, and we didn't have nearly as many desertions in those ports.

One evening while my partner and I were cruising around the waterfront checking the bars and bawdy houses, we got a call from the Galveston Police Department to assist their officers responding to a *riot* on one of the ships. We arrived at the ship about the same time as the police, and we went aboard with several policemen. The *riot* was more of a shouting match than a battle, and the root of the matter was quickly determined. Two of the local *ladies-of-the-night* had met some of the ship's crewmembers in one of the waterfront bars, and the sailors had invited the *ladies* to the ship for a *party*. Everything was going along fine until a dispute arose over the *ladies'* charges for various *party favors*. The sailors considered the charges to be exorbitant, and they were raising a fuss. Apparently, the negotiations got louder and louder until someone called the police.

The dispute was quickly resolved by the police who removed the *ladies*, one black *lady* and one white *lady*, from the ship. After placing the *ladies* in the back seat of his patrol car, one of the policemen, a big, burly black man, leaned over the front seat and said, "Women! What's the matter with you? You ought to be ashamed! Don't you know that things like this can cause an international commotion?" My partner and I hurried back to our car before we broke-out laughing. For weeks afterward we reminded each other not to do anything that might cause an *international commotion*.

One day the Beaumont Police called and asked for our assistance to interview four Spanish crewmen suspected of involvement in a burglary. The crewmen had allegedly broken into a warehouse and stolen a number of transistor radios, which had not been recovered by the police. The crewmen spoke very little English, and the police wanted to know what happened to the radios.

My partner and I each took one crewman out of the holding cell and began our interrogations at desks on opposite sides of the squad-room. I had just finished identifying myself to the individual that I was going to question when out of the corner of my eye I noticed one of the detectives, a six-foot-four East Texas cowboy, walking around the room glaring at the Spanish sailors. I didn't pay him much attention, and I went on with my questioning. Suddenly, he pulled-out an oversized blackjack, the biggest old blackjack I've ever seen, and he slammed it down on a desktop in the middle of the room. I jumped a couple of inches, and the crewman that I was talking to jumped about a foot. The detective then calmly walked out of the office without saying a word.

When things settled down, the crewmen couldn't talk fast enough. They admitted the burglary and that they had hidden the radios, and they offered to show us where they were hidden. They had wrapped the radios in plastic, put them into two burlap bags along with some rocks for weight, tied the bags with rope, and sank them in the water near the gangway of their ship. They intended to recover them just before the ship sailed.

The local district attorney declined prosecution, and we returned the crewmen to their ship and ordered them detained-on-board. Some interrogation techniques work better than others, I suppose.

In May of 1961, the Attorney General ordered a detail of three hundred fifty Border Patrol officers to assist the United States Marshals in quelling racial disturbances at Oxford, Mississippi, and in Montgomery and Selma, Alabama. The entire compliment of the Galveston station, with the exception of me, was assigned to the detail. I was left behind alone to keep the station open.

Between May and August of 1961, there were four hijackings of commercial airliners in the United States, all of them by mentally unstable political dissidents. On August 10th, President Kennedy announced on the national news networks that U.S. Border Patrol officers would be assigned to protect commercial airplanes in flight and prevent future attempts at hijacking.

Twelve hours later, armed Border Patrol officers were in the sky; they were the first of the *sky marshals*. Over the next three months, fifty officers a day were accompanying ninety-two flights a day. Several Galveston officers were assigned flights out of Houston. We dressed in plain clothes and carried a snub-nosed revolver, handcuffs, and the small, first generation, CN-3 teargas pens. Before Federal Aviation Agency officers took over and relieved us in October, Border Patrol officers had flown on 1,310 commercial flights and traveled more than 1,700,000 air miles without incident.

Not all of our activity at Galveston was enjoyable. One day a ship caught fire out in *the roads*, and a number of Chinese crewmen were trapped on the fantail. The ship was still under way, and the flames were approaching the fantail rapidly. The frightened crewmen began to leap into the water to escape the flames. Many of them were without life jackets, and they were pulled under by the force of the ships screws and drowned. A few were rescued and survived. We were asked to take the surviving crewmen to the city morgue and try to identify the bodies that were recovered by the Coast Guard and account for all of the crewmen listed on the ship's manifest. It wasn't a pleasant task.

September 11th is only another day of the year on the calendar, but in the year 2001 it went down in history as perhaps the second most infamous event in American history. It wasn't a good day in 1961 in Galveston, Texas, either. It was the day Hurricane Carla came ashore.

Carla was a nasty lady! The storm stalled off Matagorda Island, southwest of Galveston, on the Ninth day of September. We started to feel the impact of winds and rising tides almost immediately, and the population was being encouraged to evacuate before the full force of the storm struck. Border Patrol families living on the mainland stayed at home, and those of us living on the island, including the Brandemuehls, the Gustafsons, and the Briens, took refuge in the Border Patrol and INS offices on the second floor of the Federal Building in downtown Galveston.

We were later joined in our haven in the Federal Building by Dan Rather and his TV crew. As it turned out, it was his coverage of Hurricane Carla that put Dan Rather on the fast track to prominence in the national news media.

As the storm intensified, the water began to rise throughout a major portion of the city. The Gustafsons were living in a trailer park on the west end of the island. When we received reports of flooding two to three feet in that area, we decided to try to retrieve some of their belongings before they were destroyed. We were able to drive to within four or five city blocks of the trailer park, but then we had to wade the rest of the way. By the time we got there, the water was waist high in the street at there was about a foot of water in the Gustafson's trailer. We put everything in the trailer up as high as we could, gathered up Gus's guns and important papers, and waded back to our vehicle.

By the time we got back to the Federal Building the streets downtown were flooding. We parked our personal vehicles and the Border Patrol vehicles on the ramp behind the building in hopes of keeping them dry.

Within a few hours the island was completely cut off from the mainland, all of the streets downtown were flooded and impassable, and many homes and buildings were flooded. Almost all public services, police, fire, and transportation were seriously curtailed.

About noon on the Tenth a small shrimp boat carefully made its way up the street in front of the Federal Building and tied up to a parking meter.

When the storm came ashore on the eleventh, it was a category five hurricane with winds that reached 150 miles an hour. All of the electricity on the island was knocked-out, and the fresh water supply was critical. The Galveston Police advised us that their entire fleet of vehicles was inoperable, as were their two-way radios. Our Border Patrol vehicles, parked on the ramp behind the Federal Building were still above the water, and for some time the radios in our patrol cars were the only law enforcement communications link to the mainland.

The mainland had not faired much better than the island, and Border Patrol officers there were busy trying to protect their families and helping emergency crews where and when they could.

After being buffeted by Carla's winds and flooded by the rising sea for about twelve hours, the island was battered by a series of twisters that did extensive damage to everything in their path. We emerged from our temporary haven to a scene of massive destruction and despair. Then to make matters worse, the looters came in droves; the city was infested with thieves.

Our two Border Patrol vehicles survived the storm in good condition, but the streets were so cluttered with mud and debris that we couldn't get around very well. We did make it out to the Galveston Hotel on the seawall, where a number of people had sought refuge from the storm only to be stranded in its aftermath. We transported a number of them back to their homes in the city, an unpleasant task. Some of these folks had lost everything, their entire homes and everything in them, and others arrived to find various levels of saltwater and mud in their homes. It was a sad and disheartening time.

The day after the hurricane, the Texas National Guard moved in and helped the police to restore order and gain control over the looters. The sun appeared again in the sky. The electric power came back on and with it the fresh water supply. Everyone breathed a sigh of relief; it was over.

The resilience and *can do* spirit of the American people, always apparent at the scene of a disaster, took over and they began to cleanup and rebuild. It was probably because of the advance warning and the number of people who evacuated before the storm hit that there was very little loss of life from Hurricane Carla. It was bad, but it could have been worse.

The Border Patrol was still a *mobile organization*, and some of the officers who were there when I arrived moved on to bigger and better things. Everett Gustafson, Carl Judkins, Bob Murray, Hugh Brien, Howard Whitworth, Larry Teverbaugh, Don Baunfield and Henry McCormack came in to replace those who left.

Don Jordan was transferred to the Northeast Regional Office, where he became Assistant Regional Commissioner for Border Patrol. H.K. Nettle replaced him in Galveston as station senior. His first name was

Harold, but I never heard him addressed in any way other than as "H. K." He was known throughout the Service by his initials; he never told me why.

Many of the officers that I worked with in Galveston went on to middle and high level management positions in the Service before they retired; Don Day preceded me as Assistant Commissioner for Border Patrol, and Hugh Brien replaced me in that position when I retired. Larry Teverbaugh rose to the rank of Chief Patrol Agent. Galveston must have been a good training ground.

Galveston, Oh Galveston; I have a lot of fond memories of the island, my time there, and the people that I knew there. I measure life by the people that I meet along the way, and I've had a full measure with the people that I served with in the Border Patrol and the Immigration and Naturalization Service.

\+ + + + + + +

A Guy Could Get Hurt In This Job

by

Hank Henderson

It was July 16, 1958; I'll never forget the date. I was stationed in Galveston, Texas. The day had started like most summer days on the Texas Gulf Coast, hot and humid.

Galveston was considered to be primarily a Crewman Control station, and just about everyone in the station that day, myself included, had gone to Houston to search an Italian freighter, the *S.S. Francisco Morosine*, for stowaways. It was something that all of us had done many times before, and I wasn't expecting anything unusual to mark the date in my memory. These things always happen when you least expect it.

Miles Adams and I were working together, and we started to search the ship's number two hold. The hatch was covered on the weather deck, but there was a small inspection hatch, about three feet square, directly over a vertical ladder leading down into the various cargo holds on the lower decks within the ship. Miles and I could easily climb through the inspection hatch, so we didn't ask the crew to remove the main hatch cover. Miles went down the ladder first, and I waited on the weather deck until he reached the bottom; we had a rule that only one man would be on a ladder at a time.

I started down the ladder when Miles signaled that he had reached the bottom. Very little light was getting into the spaces below the weather deck through the small inspection hatch, and it was about as dark as Carlsbad Caverns when the rangers turn off the lights and sing *Rock of Ages*. You can almost feel the darkness. All we had for light was our plastic two-cell explosion proof flashlights.

When I reached the first deck below the weather deck, Miles called up to me and said that he had located something suspicious. I stepped off the ladder and swung the beam of my flashlight around inside the large empty hold. The ship was in ballast, that is, there was no cargo aboard and all of the holds were empty. In the light cast by my puny two-cell flashlight I couldn't see very well, but something attracted my attention. I didn't know exactly what it was. Now I think that it might have been a man, but we'll get to that later.

When the previous cargo had been removed, the crew had stacked the hatch cover boards in a pile next to the open hatch. I stepped up on the pile of boards to get a better look around inside the empty hold. Suddenly the top board pitched up, projecting me into the open hatch.

I fell sixty feet to the bottom of the ship, and I spent the next eighty-nine days in Houston's St. Joseph's Hospital hanging by my heels. At first the doctors doubted that I would ever walk again, but being the stubborn cuss that I am, three months later I stumbled out of the hospital on my feet. I almost immediately passed-out on the sidewalk in front of the hospital, but I *did* walk out!

Immediately after my fall, I had very little memory of what happened; I assumed that I had just lost my balance and fallen into the void, but as time passed, my memory of the details began to return. I remembered that as I fell, in the beam of my flashlight, I got a glimpse of a man at the end of the board that I was standing on; he was lifting it up trying to dump me off. At first I thought that I might be imagining things, reliving the incident in my dreams, so to speak. I have since learned that a temporary loss of memory is not unusual in such circumstances, nor is a return of memories of the specific details of traumatic events after months or years unusual.

It was more than a year after the accident when my memory of seeing the man at the end of the board as I fell came back to me. The reports had all been filed and the accident all but forgotten by everyone but me by that time, and I didn't bother to mention the return of my memory of the mysterious face at the end of the board to anyone.

Sometime later I learned that about a month after my fall an alien had been apprehended in Kansas City who claimed to have entered the United States as a stowaway on the ship tied-up directly ahead of the *S.S. Francisco Morosine* on the day of my accident. At about the same time that I fell, a longshoreman fell on that ship and was killed. The alien claimed that he managed to escape from the ship and the dock area in the confusion caused by the fatal accident. I've often wondered if he was the man who I saw at the end of the board when I was falling.

I eventually went back to full Border Patrol duty, but I still have some residual problems from the accident. I lost a lot of the strength in my right arm, but over the years I've learned to compensate and live with my limitations. I had to carry my sidearm on my left side the rest of my career and learn to shoot with my left hand, but I managed.

I worked six and a half years searching ships on the Texas Gulf Coast, and I only had the one accident, which I survived in fairly good shape. I was lucky.

In January of 1962 I was promoted to supervisor and transferred to Warroad, Minnesota, as the station senior. My sole ambition in the Border Patrol had been to lead my own station, and I was delighted with the transfer and promotion.

As compared to the Texas Gulf Coast, I led a quiet and peaceful life in Warroad for several years, but nothing lasts forever. In March of 1972 my peace and quiet suddenly got noisy and anything but peaceful. In retrospect, I am lucky to have survived that one, too.

Bill Tuffley and I were patrolling near Warroad when we got a call advising us that two men had stolen a car in International Falls, kidnapped the driver and placed him in the trunk of the car, and were headed west toward Warroad. They were considered armed and dangerous, and we were advised to proceed with caution.

We were armed only with our sidearms at the time, so we immediately returned to the office where I told Bill to grab a shotgun. We then proceeded to the Warroad River Bridge, about the middle of town, where we met a local sheriff's deputy who had gotten the same call.

The bridge was being rebuilt, and the old bridge was closed and torn down. A temporary bypass using large concrete culverts had been constructed around the site where the new bridge was under construction, and the detour was barely wide enough for two cars to pass each other going in opposite directions. It was an ideal place to set up a roadblock. The deputy sheriff parked his car across the detour road at the far end, and we waited off the road a short distance east of the bridge. The plan was to let the bad guys drive onto the detour road and we would come in behind them, trapping them between us and the sheriff's car blocking the road. Any reasonable and responsible person would give-up at that point and we could take them into custody without anyone getting hurt. Unfortunately, these two weren't reasonable and responsible persons.

While we were setting up the roadblock, we got a call advising us that the hostage had called the sheriff's department to report that he was all right, that the fugitives had released him, and that they had continued on toward Warroad. At least the hostage was safe and out-of-the-way. That was a load off my mind; we wouldn't have to worry about an innocent in the middle of a gunfight.

We didn't have to wait long before we saw the fugitives approaching the river on the highway at a high rate of speed. They could certainly see the sheriff's car blocking the road, but they weren't slowing down. When they passed us, I pulled in behind them and chased them onto the detour road. They swerved onto the temporary road, almost lost control, and kept on going. They hit the rear end of the sheriff's car and knocked it out of the way. Thankfully, the deputy had taken cover behind a concrete bridge abutment, and he was not behind the car. The sheriff's car spun around in the road from the impact and blocked our pursuit until the deputy could get in and pull it out of the way.

When the sheriff's car was out of the way, we took off in pursuit of the fugitives, with the sheriff's deputy following behind us in his damaged patrol car. Within a mile or so we caught up to the fugitives' stolen car, and one of them began shooting at us through the back window of car with what we later determined to be a .308 caliber rifle. He blew the back window out of the stolen car with the first shot, which also hit our windshield. The pursuit continued at high speeds, at times in excess of a hundred miles an hour, toward the Canadian border, about six miles north of town.

Throughout the pursuit, one of the fugitives continued shooting at us with the rifle. Somehow he managed to get into the trunk of the vehicle, and several times he fired at us blindly through the trunk lid. Then he returned to the rear window and continued firing from that position. He was obviously a trained and accomplished marksman. We later counted twenty-one hits on our patrol car, three of which had hit the windshield. We could actually see the bullets coming toward us, which was an odd and scary sight to be sure. Fortunately, probably because of the speed we were traveling and the bullets striking the car at odd angles, most of the lead bullets did not penetrate the car's body and they only cracked the windshield.

It seemed probable that the fugitives were headed toward the border and intended to flee into Canada. I called Immigrant Inspector Mike Hackett at the U.S. port-of entry on the radio and advised him of the circumstances. I also asked him to call the doctor in Warroad and have him proceed to the port-of-entry with an ambulance, as it was very possible that someone was going to be hurt before this was over. He called the Canadians and the doctor, and then he got the Customs' revolver out of the safe where it was kept. Immigration officers at ports-of-entry were not armed at that time, but Mike had spent years in the Border Patrol, and he knew how to handle a gun.

When the fugitives arrived at the Canadian border, it was obvious from their high rate of speed that they had no intention of stopping for inspection or anything else. Mike Hackett took careful aim with the .38 Special revolver, fired two shots, and blew-out the right front tire on the stolen car, sending the car into an uncontrolled spin. It came to a sliding stop near one of the concrete international boundary markers. Later examination of the vehicle revealed the two bullets from Mike Hackett's revolver inside the right front tire.

We stopped the patrol car immediately behind the fugitives' stolen car, and I started to jump out. One of the fugitives fired a pistol at me at that moment, and the patrol car's seat belt probably saved my life. In the excitement, I'd forgotten to unhook the seatbelt, and when I started to get out, it caught me up short. The fugitive's bullet passed just inches short of my face. I am now a firm believer in seatbelts.

As I exited the car, I fired one shot with my left hand around the doorpost, and then without thinking, I switched hands and fired a second shot with my right hand. Although I hadn't practiced shooting with my right hand since my accident, in the stress of the moment it seemed natural. My first shot hit the man who had shot at me in the chest, and he went down immediately. The force of the .357 bullet drove him backward and across the international line into Canada.

The second fugitive was crouching and aiming a pistol at me, and I directed my second shot at him. Just as I squeezed the trigger, he stood up, and my bullet caught him in the leg. He also fell into Canada, but he got up and stumbled back into the United States. He was hurting and bleeding badly, and he asked me for help. I put him into the patrol car and took him to the hospital in Warroad. Actually, this was not a completely humanitarian act on my part. I wanted to get him away from the scene as soon as possible and avoid any conflict with the Canadian Mounties over who would take custody.

Bill Tuffley was also shooting at the fugitives at the international boundary, and at first we didn't know who had shot who. Although I was almost certain that my shots had both found their mark, the wound to the dead fugitive was such that some of the people on the scene believed that Tuffley had shot him in the back with the shotgun. The coroner resolved the issue; the entry wound was caused by a single bullet through the chest, but the .357 round had virtually blown the man's heart out through his back. The exit wound did, in fact, look like a shotgun wound, but it wasn't.

Bill Tuffley and I attended the coroner's inquest in Steinbeck, Manitoba, Canada. The Canadian coroner found: "the deceased contributed to his own death by refusing to obey the lawful orders of a United States Border Patrolman."

Both fugitives were later determined to be active duty United States Marines from Detroit Lakes, Minnesota, who were home on leave. One had just returned from a year in Vietnam, and the other was a military policeman with orders to go to Vietnam at the end of his leave. For some reason known only to them, they had embarked on a several days long crime spree of robbery, burglary, and assault before we brought it to an end in Warroad. Before they stole the automobile and kidnapped its owner in International Falls, they had robbed a liquor store and burglarized a sporting goods store, where they undoubtedly obtained the guns and ammunition that they used against us.

The survivor was ultimately convicted of a variety of crimes and sentenced to thirty years in prison. While he was awaiting trial in International Falls, he escaped from jail. Another inmate reported that he had said he intended to go to Warroad and "get" me. The sheriff in International Falls took the threat seriously and notified me and the sheriff's office in Warroad. Bill Tuffley and I went east along the highway to International Falls hoping to locate the escapee before he reached the town; the last thing that we wanted was another shoot-out in town. Fortunately, an off-duty sheriff's deputy recognized him walking along the highway. He was taken back into custody and subsequently served his entire thirty-year sentence.

Later I received word that some family members of the dead man were planning to come after me for revenge. As it happened, a cousin of the man was the Chief Deputy Sheriff in Grand Rapids, Minnesota. He was made aware of the family's plans, and he convinced them in no uncertain terms to abandon any ideas of revenge.

Bill Tuffley, Mike Hackett, and I received commendations from the Regional Commissioner at a ceremony at the Warroad Border Patrol station a few months after the incident.

Yes, it's true! A guy could get hurt in this job.

Goodbye, Mama!

by

Alvin Braunstein

The word *phenomenon* has always been hard for me to pronounce, but I'll use it anyway. It best describes something that I experienced back in 1957 when I was a trainee Border Patrol Inspector in Del Rio, Texas.

The Chief Patrol Inspector was Edwin Dorn, and he liked to call trainees into his office individually and size them up. When my turn came, he quickly discovered that I was a *city boy* from San Antonio, Texas, and he started questioning me about my knowledge of firearms. I admitted that I had never handled a pistol in my life, which didn't seem to please him a lot. He nodded his head, and then he said, "You know, it would be pretty bad if you got shot while out there working the line, but let me tell you, it would be a hell of a lot worse if *you* accidentally shot someone out there." That's all it took for me, those few words, and from then on I treated my .38 caliber revolver with the utmost of respect.

I worried about accidentally shooting someone every time that I strapped on my gun to go to work. I suppose that I developed some kind of an irrational concern about it, so much so that I did the unmentionable.....I carried the pistol unloaded.

Several weeks after my talk with the chief, I was working with the sector firearms training officer, Bob Bohks, and it didn't take him long to notice that my weapon wasn't loaded. Bob was the kind of guy who liked to illustrate his instructions with something like, "Now let's both quick-draw on that tin can over there and see who can get off the first shot." We all know who got off the first and only shot, and you can imagine the choice words of advice that Mr. Bohks had for me.

Bob assumed that I had taken his advice to heart, and we never mentioned the incident again, until forty-five years later when we were both retired and reminiscing together about *the old days*. That's when I told him that I hadn't taken his advice that day; I'd continued working with an empty gun until one night I was working with Wesley Shaw, and he caught me red-handed. He was nowhere near as nice and polite about it as Bob Bohks had been. He chewed me out good, he covered everything I had done that night and then some, and he concluded that the only thing I'd done right was not slamming the jeep door when I got out to open a rancher's gate. When I thought that he was done, he added, "But you might be the only trainee that I ever met who isn't gun happy." That helped a little, but I was smarting a bit over the ass-chewing he'd given me, and Wes and I didn't say much to each other the rest of that shift.

About ten o'clock that night, we were still-watching a popular crossing point on the Rio Grande.

It was a dark night, hardly any moonlight at all. It was quiet, and there was no wind to speak of. We were both concentrating on glassing with binoculars trying to spot potential crossers on the other side. Suddenly, a flash of bright white light blinded me for a few seconds. "What the hell was that?" I blurted out.

"What the hell was what?" Shaw replied, sounding a little disgusted.

I kept my mouth shut. Maybe I'd just imagined it. I was still a trainee, subject to the effects of C and E –conduct and efficiency – reports written periodically by senior officers, and I couldn't afford to get on the bad side of anybody. I remember looking at my watch, it was exactly 10:05 P.M., and I went back to glassing the opposite bank of the river. At midnight, we called it a night, and I went home and went to bed.

The next morning, my wife woke me up telling me that Jessie Allen, a P.I. who lived next door to us, wanted to talk to me. Jessie came into the bedroom and hee-hawed around for a while before he got around to the purpose of his early morning visit: my mother had passed away the night before. My wife knew about it, but she didn't have the heart to tell me, and she had asked Jessie to break the news to me.

I took the news pretty hard, and I cried. I was the youngest of eight children, and I had a special relationship with my mother; she never stopped babying me. When I'd visit my parents, Mom would always call me her baby. And Dad would say, "Yeah, your baby elephant!"

I later discovered that my mother had died at five minutes after ten in the evening, exactly the time that the bright white light had blinded me on the riverbank. Coincidence? I don't know; I can't explain it. But over the years whenever the subject of unexplainable phenomena comes up in conversation, I always remember that night. I believe that it was my Mom telling me goodbye.

Goodbye mama; I miss you.

\+ + + + + + +

Detail to Langtry
by
W.O. "Dub" Covington

I was stationed in Sonora, Texas, in the Del Rio Sector, in 1959. Sonora was a great duty station. There was plenty of activity, and either the *wets* or the other officers that I worked with kept things lively. Nevertheless, every now and again someone was singled out and sent on detail to Langtry, which was situated down on the Rio Grande River.

Of course, everyone has heard of Langtry; although, not many people have been there. In years past, Langtry was the stompin' ground of the notorious Judge Roy Bean, *the Law West of the Pecos*.

I was tagged to go to Langtry with a probationer named Kal Sapero from the Comstock station. A detail to Langtry was for fourteen days at a stretch, and we were expected to work all fourteen days – in those days extra work days just added to your U.O.T. (A.U.O.) hours and didn't put any more money in your pocket.

There were no hotels or motels and no restaurants or fast-food places anywhere near Langtry, only one dinghy beer joint that we called *We-too's*, or something like that. I don't remember the exact name. I do remember that the walls behind and over the bar were covered with rattlesnake skins stretched and tacked to boards. The hides were probably stretched while they were wet to make the snakes appear to have been bigger than they actually were in life. Neither Kal nor I drank much beer, but we dropped in a few times to look the place over. It wasn't a place to eat, though, and we didn't spend much time there.

The Border Patrol had a travel trailer set up in Langtry for us to live in, and we'd have to do our own cooking. So Kal and I got together and bought our groceries for the two weeks before we left home.

Once we got settled in the trailer, we set out to explore the country in the old cloth-topped Jeep provided by the Border Patrol. We amused ourselves by shooting rattlesnakes along the roads. The country seemed to be alive with them everywhere we went. I shot one on the ground right in front of Kal's feet.

At night we'd go down to Chema Vega and lay-in on the river. All the way down and all the way back, we'd see dozens of rattlers and scorpions along the road. They have those big *Vinegaroones* – some folks call them *whip scorpions* – down there. The Mexicans call them *gente de la noche* (people of the night). Unlike the little desert scorpions that can give you a nasty sting, the *Vinegaroones* are harmless, but they're big and they look fierce. Harmless or not, if one crawls up your leg in the dark, it will get your attention in a hurry. It's a scary feeling.

About ten o'clock one night we received a radio call from sector headquarters in Del Rio informing us that a group of thirteen *wets* would soon be crossing the river, and they were expected to pass under the first bridge on Highway 90 west of Langtry on their way north. We were to intercept and apprehend them.

Kal and I left our Jeep about a quarter of a mile from the bridge and walked the rest of the way. A dry creek ran under the bridge, and we hid along its bank north of the bridge. We expected the group to walk through the tunnel under the bridge and follow the dry creek bed on north. Kal laid-in about fifty yards north of me along the dry creek. When all of the *wets* passed by me, I would jump out behind them, and Kal would jump out in front of them. We'd have them trapped between the banks of the creek, and they couldn't scatter and get away. At least that was the plan, but all such plans seem to have a way of going awry.

We remained in our hiding places, among the snakes, spiders, skunks, wild Javelina pigs, and Lord-only-knows what else, until after midnight without seeing or hearing a thing. Then suddenly we heard what sounded like a stampede of wild cows over the rocks and through the underbrush south of the bridge. It lasted for just a few minutes, and then all was quiet again. The *wets* had stopped in the tunnel under the bridge, and they were sitting down.

Kal crawled the fifty yards over to me and said, "What do we do now?"

I told him: "We'll just join them under the bridge and arrest everybody. The next time a truck comes over the hill its headlights will give us enough light to see where we're going, but the aliens won't be able to see us coming. And the noise the truck makes will mask any noise that we make running toward them." It seemed like a good idea to me. Kal was still on probation, and he was willing to go along with almost anything.

We waited about forty-five minutes before we saw the headlights of a truck coming over the hill, and we got ready. When the truck's headlights gave us enough light to see where we were running, we both jumped into the creek bed and ran toward the bridge…right into a wire fence across the creek where it went under the bridge. I was in the lead, and I tried to jump the fence. I didn't quite make it. I caught the toe of my boot on the fence, and I sprawled on my hands and knees right into the middle of the Mexicans. Most of them were as startled as I, and they didn't move. When I regained my feet, I shouted in Spanish, "Don't move! You are under arrest!"

One young man scampered on his hands and knees back under the bridge toward Mexico, but Kal caught up with him before he got very far, and I saw another one run out of the other end of the tunnel. I stayed with the aliens that we had in custody while Kal went looking for the one who had escaped.

He found the escapee a short distance away on Son Henderson's ranch. The alien had run headlong into a barbed wire fence and tangled himself up in the wire. Kal had to untangle him before he could arrest him.

The *wet* had made a mess of a section of Son Henderson's fence, but we had to leave it as it was that night. Kal and I went back the following day and repaired the damage.

We had thirteen *wets* in custody; no one had gotten away. Kal walked back to get the Jeep while I guarded the Mexicans. When he got back, we took our prisoners to a service station in Langtry to wait for transportation from Del Rio to take them off our hands. We bought each of them a soda pop while we waited.

Of course, the money for the soda pop came out of our pockets.

While we were waiting, I talked to the *wets*, and one of them told me that when I fell in among them he thought the truck had run off the bridge and it was coming down on them. He was too frightened to run.

Later that morning, I asked Kal how many snakes and critters he'd seen in the creek bed while he was hiding and when he came crawling down to join me. He just grunted and said, "I tried to put them out of my mind."

It was after four in the morning when we got back to the trailer and crawled in our bunks. We slept-in the next morning, but after we got up and had some breakfast, we headed back to Chema Vega to lay-in on the river. That's how it was in those days.

Kal Sapero was a fine fellow, and we had a good time down there on the river together. I don't know where he is now. He left the Border Patrol and transferred to Investigations in Los Angeles, and then I heard that he'd later on transferred to Investigations in Phoenix. I suppose, like the rest of us, he's retired now. *Mi buen companero,* Kal, if you read this, *Que tal? Pase por aqui, amigo, si puede.*

\+ \+ \+ \+ \+ \+ \+

A Dog's Life

by

Jerry Dahlberg

I worked with a dog for a time when I was a young Patrol Inspector stationed in McAllen, Texas, in the early nineteen fifties. Napper was the dog's name, and he was one of the best partners I ever had.

Napper was a Doberman Pincher that had been given to the Border Patrol by Joe and Ellen Miranda when he was little more than a pup. Joe was a Patrol Inspector in McAllen at the time. He was also a survivor of the Bataan Death March in World War II, but that's another story.

Elger 'Doc' Holiday trained Napper for Border Patrol work, and he did a great job. Napper never let 'em get away.

One particularly dark night, Napper and I were working alone on the Second Street canal levee south of Hidalgo, Texas. We were hidden in the weeds alongside the trail that leads from the river near Reynosa, Mexico. Directly behind us, only a few yards away, was a small Mexican cemetery. It was just a few graves in a small plot of land, what the Mexicans down there refer to as a *campo santo*.

We hadn't been there very long when a figure carrying a bag approached us along the trail. It was too dark to see him clearly, but I was sure he was a *mojado*; nobody else would have been using that trail at that time of night. I put a finger on Napper's nose to signal to him to be still and be quiet, and we waited.

The Mexican obviously knew the country, and he knew the *campo santo* was there. I could see him turn his head to the side and quicken his pace as he passed. He was clearly uncomfortable being so near to a cemetery at night, and I couldn't help but snicker under my breath. While I was enjoying myself giggling like a schoolgirl at the Mexican's fright, I must have let my finger slip off Napper's nose. He let out a howl that would have been the envy of any Werewolf in old London town. It even made *me* shiver, and I had both hands on its source.

The Mexican in the trail jumped two feet straight up. His *trique* bag with all of his belongings for his trip to *El Norte* went one way and his hat went the other. He took off running back the way he had come like the devil was after him with a pitchfork. Napper immediately took off after him pulling me along by the leash faster than I thought I could run.

I knew the Mexican wasn't going to get very far at night on the rough trail at the speed he was running, and it wasn't long until we found him. He had tripped over something on the trail in the dark, and he was sprawled out, face down in the fine, sandy soil. The wind had been knocked out of him by the fall, and he was moaning, but his legs were still pumping and his arms were clutching at the ground as though he were trying to swim.

When we came upon him, I shouted, "*Migracion!*" And I pulled Napper back with the leash and got him under control at my side. I could see the relief wash over the face of that Mexican; he was just a boy in his early twenties. He stuttered through tears, "*Gracias a Dios! Yo pensaba heran un espectro!*" Thank God, it's just *La Migra*! The poor fella had thought ol' Napper was a ghost. I don't imagine that he used that trail often at night after that experience.

\+ + + + + + +

John Evangelist,
Border Patrol Pilot

An autobiography

John Evangelist was a friend of mine. I first met him in 1961 when he was the sector pilot in Grand Forks, North Dakota, and I was a Patrol Inspector in Grand Marias, Minnesota. He would fly over to Grand Marias occasionally in the Border Patrol airplane, pick me up and take me with him on his patrol of the border lakes and out to Isle Royale, Michigan. We never caught anybody doing anything illegal, we didn't really expect to, but it was necessary to show-the-flag to the people living in the backwoods and check in with the park rangers at Isle Royale to let everybody know that we were on-the-job and watching. I appreciated the rides; they were a welcome diversion from patrolling a lonesome highway and a stretch of the border where little of any significance ever happened. I also enjoyed John's company. He was a few years older than me; he'd been to a lot of places and seen a lot of things, and he was a born storyteller.

John learned to fly in the Navy during World War II, but he was too late to get in on the action, and he was discharged at the end of the war. He had a number of short-term jobs that didn't really interest him much after he left the Navy, including a short fling at flying crop dusters in California's Imperial Valley. I think he liked flying the dusters, but a big storm in the valley wiped out the company and all of its airplanes, and John was left without a job. At the suggestion of a friend, he applied for the Border Patrol; although, helater admitted that he didn't know much about the Border Patrol at the time. He was accepted, and .....well, let's let John tell it.

GB

I got into the Border Patrol on June 27, 1955, in the sixty-first session of the Border Patrol Academy. I almost didn't pass the physical; I had a cavity in one of my back teeth. I had to have it filled before the doctor would pass me. I thought about having it pulled, but that would have left me with a gap between two of my back teeth, which would have disqualified me for the Border Patrol. That's how picky they were in those days.

There was a lot of physical training at the academy, and I was thirty-two years old, the oldest in my class. Most of the others were in their early twenties; they called me *Pop*. I've always kept myself in pretty good shape, though, and I didn't have any trouble keeping up with the kids.

When we graduated from the academy, I was sent to Fort Hancock, Texas, which was just a wide spot in the road in those days. As soon as I found a place to live, my wife and the kids joined me. They couldn't believe how primitive living was there at that time. We had to haul our drinking water from McNary, a filling station and restaurant about two miles away, because we couldn't drink the local water. It took some getting used to, but, thinking back, we enjoyed our time there, especially the kids. They soon made friends with the other kids in town, and they had a great time while we were there.

Border Patrol activity at Fort Hancock in those days was mostly sign-cutting. We didn't have a garage at the station, so we kept the government jeeps at home, and we'd go out on patrol direct from home. We had drag roads about a mile and a half from the border, and we'd pull our drags along the roads and look for sign at the same time. When we found tracks crossing the drag road, we'd drop the drag and take off following the trail. We had some long chases; sometimes we would follow the tracks for two or three days before we caught the aliens a hundred miles or more from Fort Hancock.

I remember one time that we chased these two Mexicans for two days. When we finally caught them, they were sitting on their haunches eating a rabbit that they had caught. They had a small cooking fire, and they had skinned and gutted the rabbit, but they were too hungry to wait for it to cook. They were eating the meat practically raw, and the blood was dripping off their chins. I couldn't believe it; they were so….. They were starving. We shared our lunch with them.

One Sunday morning, I was gassing my jeep at the filling station, and there was another man there gassing his automobile. He smiled and said, "I didn't know P.I.s worked on Sunday."

I didn't know him, but I knew that he was another border patrolman because he'd called me a P.I. We referred to ourselves as P.I.s, *Patrol Inspectors*, but no one else ever addressed us that way. "We work seven days a week," I said, laughing, and I introduced myself.

He was Ed Parker; and he was on his way to Brownsville, Texas. He had just been appointed safety officer for the Border Patrol Air Transport division, which had its headquarters in Brownsville. We talked a while, and I asked him, "How do you get into the flying end of the Border Patrol?" I told him that I'd learned to fly in the Navy and that I had done some crop dusting in California. I didn't mention it to him, but the past few months I'd been so happy with my job in the Border Patrol that I hadn't given any thought to getting back into aviation.

He said, "If you're interested in coming on the airlift, I'll arrange a detail to Brownsville for you and give you a try-out." I thought he was kidding, but four days later I had orders to report to Brownsville for a thirty day detail.

The Border Patrol Air Transportation office was in the PanAm hanger at the Brownsville airport. I walked in and introduced myself to several of the pilots. Phil Pring, one of the senior pilots, said to me, "We're going to Chicago in the morning. Do you know anything about flying a DC-3?"

"No;" I replied. "I've never been in one in my life."

"Well, the airplane is right outside; go out there and look it over. Take the DC-3 flight manual with you, read it, and familiarize yourself with the airplane. Then meet us here in the morning."

Phil was in charge of the flight to Chicago, and I met him and his co-pilot at the airport at five o'clock the next morning. I was expecting to ride-along on the flight to Chicago and observe. Phil had something else in mind. He walked me through the pre-flight procedures, and then we climbed up into the cockpit. "Get in left seat," he said.

Wait a minute now, I thought. That's the pilot's seat. I'm not a Border Patrol pilot; I'm a GS-8 Patrol Inspector. But I climbed into the left seat and strapped myself in. Then he showed me how to start the engines; actually, he did everything, but I watched carefully so that I'd be able to do it myself the next time.

"Okay, let's taxi out," Phil said."

What? I'd never taxied a twin engine airplane. It's quite a bit different than a single engine plane. You have to run one engine up and then the other to make the zig-zag turns so that you can see ahead of the airplane. You don't use the brakes to taxi because they get hot really quick.

Anyway, I got out on the runway, and he asked the tower for clearance to take off on an instrument flight plan. When we got our clearance, he said, "Okay, let's go!"

"What? You gotta be kidding!"

"No! Go! I'll follow through with you."

I pushed the throttles forward, and we began to roll down the runway. I was having a hard time keeping the airplane going straight; I'd give the right engine a little more throttle to go left, and then the left engine a little more throttle to go right, and pretty soon I didn't have anymore throttle on either side, and I had to go to the rudder pedals. We were going down the runway this way and then that way, and Phil and his co-pilot were laughing and having a heck of a time watching me trying to get that airplane to go straight and get off the ground. We finally made it, broke ground, lifted the gear, and I flew it on to Chicago. When we got there, I had to land, and that was something else again. With Phil's help, I managed to bounce it in.

We spent the night in Chicago, and the next day we loaded the airplane with aliens. It was decided then that I would fly back to Brownsville, but it would be different this time. The airplane had been empty the day before, now there were twenty-six aliens aboard and the three of us. The airplane was much heavier; it took a longer run to take off, and I could feel the extra weight when I pushed the yoke forward to raise the tail. The airplane handled a lot differently with the added weight.

We made it back to Brownsville in one piece, and apparently I did all right. The next day I was offered a job on the airlift and a transfer to Brownsville. A week later they terminated my detail, and I went back to Fort Hancock to get my family and move to my new duty station. But I was still a Patrol Inspector, one of nine competing for six permanent jobs on the airlift.

In October of 1957, I was promoted to pilot (GS-11), and we thought that was really great. I had started in the Border Patrol at an annual salary of $3,995, and in a little more than two years I was a pilot earning close to $8,000 a year. That was good money in those days.

We had a four engine aircraft, a Douglas DC-4, that we used for trips to deport people to Europe, mostly criminals and mentally ill aliens. Some of them were goofy, crazy people, difficult to handle, but we had doctors – I suppose they were psychiatrists – and guards on board to watch them, and usually we had two or three INS Port Receptionists to act as stewardesses.

On the European flights, our route usually took us from New York to Gander, Newfoundland, where we would refuel and then fly on to Shannon, Ireland. From Shannon, we would fly to several destinations in Europe to deliver our passengers, and then we would fly to Vienna, Rome, or Athens to layover before returning to the United States. Between 1957 and 1960, I made nineteen trips to Europe in the DC-4. I got to see a lot of Europe, and I had a good time. Most of the trips were uneventful, but there was one that I remember vividly….

It was the middle of winter, and the weather in Gander was terrible when we left on our way to Shannon. About one o'clock in the morning we were out over the Atlantic about a hundred fifty miles from what was called our *equal time line*, that is, the point where it is approximately the same flying time to go on to Shannon or to go back to Gander. A fire warning light came on signaling a fire in number two engine. We were covered with ice, and we couldn't see the engine from inside the airplane. We couldn't tell if we had a fire or not, but the thing was saying *fire*, so we shut the engine down and *feather* the prop. To *feather* the propeller means to turn the individual blades so that their leading edge is pointed straight into the wind to reduce the amount of drag as much as possible. The blades then aren't being pushed by the wind to spin, and the propeller doesn't turn.

We could fly on three engines, but with the added weight of the ice covering the airplane, we couldn't maintain our altitude. We had been flying at eight thousand feet, but with the loss of power we were steadily dropping down. There was nothing below us but water, and the life expectancy of an unprotected human being in that water at that time of the year is measured in minutes, not very many minutes.

It was slightly closer to go back to Gander, so we checked the weather there by radio. Gander was reporting zero ceiling and zero visibility, and it wasn't expected to get any better any time soon. In other words, you couldn't see a thing. Shannon reported a fifteen hundred foot broken ceiling and two miles visibility with light rain. Even though it was a little farther, we decided to continue on to Shannon.

In the beginning, we tried to hold our altitude, but the airplane began to shudder, which means that it was about to stall, which means that it was going to fall out of the sky pretty soon, and that's something that you obviously don't want to happen. We put the nose down slightly to gain a little air speed, and it stopped shuddering.

Five hours later we were still flying but slowly dropping down toward the sea. I was flying the co-pilot's seat on that flight; John Wright was in charge. Ordinarily, we would fly for five hours and then let the relief crew have it for five hours while we got some rest, but under those conditions, John and I stayed at the controls. We were just about ready to start throwing stuff out of the airplane to lighten our load when we realized that we were maintaining altitude at about eight hundred feet. We must have gone through some rain or something and lost some of the ice. So we turned the airplane over to the other crew and got some sleep. When I woke up, the sun was shining through the little porthole above my berth. We were back up to seven thousand feet and approaching Shannon. The crisis was over.

When we weren't off on a European trip, we were flying all over the United States in DC-3s or C-46s transporting aliens and federal prison inmates. It was a good job, and I enjoyed it, but I was away from home a lot of the time, and my children were growing up. They were playing football and other sports, and I was missing it all. So I decided that it was time to get a job where I could be home every night, or at least most nights. Bill Graham was the sector pilot in Grand Forks, North Dakota, and he wanted to come back to the airlift, so we swapped positions.

When I got to Grand Forks, I discovered that my patrol area was from Sandusky, Ohio, to Seattle, Washington; I had that whole stretch of the northern border to patrol, just one airplane and me. I wouldn't be home *every* night. There were some overnight trips and some week-long details, but I wasn't away nearly as much as I had been on the airlift.

I flew the DeHavilland Beaver in Grand Forks. It was a single engine, but a big airplane, and it was setup to be amphibious. In the summer it carried pontoons so that I could land on water if need be, or I could drop the wheels down through holes in the pontoons and land on the ground. In winter, I replaced the pontoons with skis that would drop down over the wheels if I needed to land on snow or ice. It was a great airplane and a lot of fun to fly.

In August of 1964, I transferred to El Centro, California. Here in El Centro, Border Patrol flying is low and slow, sometimes as low as fifty feet off the ground, looking for aliens on the ground and looking for the footprints of smugglers and aliens entering the United States illegally.

It's surprising what you can see from the air; you can actually follow faint footprints in the sand for miles and miles if you know what you're doing. It takes a while to learn to track from the air, to distinguish between human and animal tracks, but once you learn how, you can do a pretty effective job much faster than on the ground.

I loved my job in El Centro. We flew Super Cubs most of the time, and it was like going hunting every day, only we weren't hunting wild animals; we were hunting people.

On a typical day in El Centro there were two pilots on duty. We would meet at sector headquarters at five o'clock in the morning and check with the radio operator to see what was going on. If there was a chase going on somewhere, and an airplane would help, one or both of us would join in. If it was quiet, we would both fly down to Calexico, and then one of us would go east and one west looking for alien crossers or tracks leading across the border from Mexico. If we spotted people, we'd call a ground unit in to take them into custody. If we spotted tracks leading north, we'd coordinate with ground units, and the chase was on.

People don't believe you when you say, "I can track a guy across the desert." But it's true; once you learn how to do it. Even though I don't see his footprints on hard ground for two miles or more, I can go ahead to a dry wash that I know he will have to cross and pick up the tracks again in the soft sand. Then I'll jump ahead another couple of miles and cut another dry wash. If he hasn't crossed that wash, I know that he's somewhere between the two washes that I've already cut, and I start looking for him. Most of the time, I'll find him.

Sign-cutting, whether from the air or on the ground, is an art; it's a challenge, and it's satisfying and great fun once you perfect your skill.

I worked in El Centro for thirteen years before I retired, and there were a number of memorable incidents, some with happy endings and some not so happy.

Early one morning, I found the tracks of six people leading from the border right out across the Navy bombing range. I called the control tower at the El Centro Naval Air Station on the radio and asked, "Are you going to be doing any bombing today? I've got six aliens walking across the range."

The tower replied, "Not now, but they will start bombing about ten o'clock."

We had to get those aliens off the range before the bombing started, and we only had a couple of hours to find them and get them out of there. I told the Navy tower, "I'll be over the range, and I'll let you know when I'm clear. I will be out of there before ten o'clock." To make a long story short, I found them and we got a unit out there to remove them before the Navy started bombing. If I hadn't cut their tracks going in and found them in time, the ending of this story might have been different.

Another time, I was flying the railroad tracks near Niland when I spotted these two boys walking alone the tracks. They evidently knew the Border

Patrol airplane when they saw it, and as soon as they saw me they tried to hide. I knew right where they were, and I tried to get a ground unit to come and pick them up, but there was no one available. So I landed on a dirt road and walked back to where they were hiding. They were just youngsters; one was about eleven years old and the other was about nine. I asked them if they would like a ride in the airplane, and they were real excited about it. They were so small that I strapped them into one seat together and off we went. As we flew back to El Centro, I pointed out things on the ground to them, and they just had a great time. I suppose that they were sent back to Mexicali that afternoon, but they'd had an adventure not shared by many Mexican kids.

Carl Ott was a Border Patrol pilot who I worked with a lot in El Centro. One morning I was flying along the Coachella Canal when I spotted Carl's Border Patrol airplane parked on the canal bank. I assumed that he had had engine trouble, so I landed on the canal road and taxied my airplane up to where Carl was standing. He didn't have engine problems.

Carl had been flying the canal when he spotted a little *burro* apparently stuck in the mud. He had landed to try to rescue the little animal, but he couldn't get him out of the mud by himself. The *burro* was just a little fella, about the size of a dog, and cute as can be. I put my finger on his nose, and he took it into his mouth and started sucking on it; he was just a baby. Between the two of us, Carl and I got him out of the mud and up on the road. We intended to leave him there, and Carl got into his plane and left. I started to leave, but the little guy wouldn't get out of the way. I was afraid that he would get into the propeller when I started the engine. So I tied his legs with a piece of rope, lifted him into the back seat of the airplane, strapped him down with the seat belts, and we took off.

When I got back to El Centro, I put him in my car and took him to Carl Ott's house. Carl's kids went crazy over the cute little fella. They kept him as long as they could, but Carl lived in town, and when the *burro* got older and started braying all night, keeping the neighbors awake, he had to go. Carl gave him to a farmer who had several other *burros*.

Keith Riley was his name, and he was just a little boy, maybe five or six years old. He had wandered away from a Methodist Church picnic in the desert near Mount Signal in 1969, and he had apparently gotten lost. We looked and looked and looked for that boy, the sheriff's rescue team, the Border Patrol in the air and on the ground, Mexican firemen, *the bomberos*, we even brought a helicopter in to look for him. We looked for two long days, but we couldn't find any sign of him.

It was the Mexican *bomberos* who finally found him. He had gotten into the shale on the east side of the mountain, fallen a long way down a steep slope, and landed in a crack between two rocks. I was impossible to see him from the air. The fall hadn't killed him; the firemen could see where he had thrashed around in the loose shale before he died. It was a sad, tragic thing.

In October of 1974, Border Patrol agents on the ground intercepted a group of Mexican people trying to cross the border in real rough country west of Mount Signal. The country out there is so rough that we referred to it as *the bad lands*. The people spotted the officers before they were close enough to apprehend them, and they ran back across the border and hid in Mexico. The next night, after dark, they tried crossing the border again, but they got lost and ran out of water. For some reason, they then left a fifteen-year-old girl in the desert to wait while the rest of them went to find water. When they returned to where they had left her, she was gone. They then turned themselves in to the Border Patrol to get help to find the missing girl. The Border Patrol and the sheriff's rescue team started looking for her on the American side, and the Mexican *bomberos* searched on the Mexican side.

At daylight, I joined the search from the air, and I found the little girl's tracks going in a southwesterly direction. It was obvious to me from the way that her trail was wandering around that she was lost. I followed her trail to a rock ledge about a quarter of a mile into Mexico, but I couldn't find her tracks leading away. The terrain was so rough there that there was no possibility of getting any kind of vehicle even close. I circled around and made a couple of passes over the spot where her tracks ended, and I spotted her shadow under the ridge. I made a pass from the other direction, and I saw her lying in the sand. I couldn't tell if she was alive or dead.

Border Patrol airplanes are equipped with a loudspeaker system for communicating with people on the ground. I turned the radio switch to *speaker* and shouted in Spanish, "Are you okay? Help is on the way! If you can hear me, wave your arms!" She slowly lifted one arm. She was alive!

The girl's brother was on foot about a mile away. I flew over him and told him on the speaker that

I had found his sister and I would direct him to where she was. It was 120 degrees in the shade that day, and there wasn't any shade, but that boy took off at a full run. I was afraid that he would drop before he reached her, but he made it with his canteen full of water.

Bill Glenn and his partner, F. J. Danforth, tried to get to the location in their Border Patrol jeep, but about a half mile away, the jeep got stuck in the sand. Bill went on afoot with another canteen full of water for the girl and Danforth stayed behind to dig the jeep out of the sand and get it moving again. Bill got to the girl about the same time as her brother.

There was nowhere close that I could land; the country was just too rough. So I went out to the highway and landed in the road. I showed the sheriff's rescue team where the girl was located, and they brought her out on the west side of Mount Signal. I saw her and talked to her; she was recovering and happy that she had been found in time. So was I! It made up a little bit for the loss of the little boy five years before.

In the years that I flew the Border Patrol airplane in El Centro, I found a lot of bodies out in the desert. They were mostly Mexicans trying to slip into the United States illegally, but I found some *gringos*, too. They had gotten out into the desert, gotten lost, and died of exposure, most of them.

I found a body one time less than a hundred yards from the Colorado River. He had probably died not knowing that lifesaving water was so close. The sun had turned the body black, and the skin was like leather. Another time I found a skeleton, all that was left of the body was bones and a little mummified flesh on the scalp. He had been a redhead; there was still some red hair hanging to the mummified skin. The local authorities finally decided that it was the body of a soldier training with Patton's army out there during World War II; he had either deserted or gotten lost and died out there in the desert.

I was tracking a group of four aliens across the desert one time, and all of a sudden their tracks divided, two went to the right and two went to the left. After a short distance, they came back together and continued on in the direction that they had been going. I made a low pass over the area and saw a skeleton on the ground; the aliens had walked up to it, seen it, walked carefully around it, and then continued on their way. I called the sheriff's office, and then I landed on old highway 80 and met the deputies. We followed the alien's tracks from the highway to where the body lay.

You never knew what you might find out in that desert. I found a bunch of motorcycles out there one time; there must have been twenty of them all together. Mostly, it was motorcycle parts, handlebars, wheels, fenders, seats, engines, and engine parts scattered around, but there were a few motorcycles still together. There were a lot of empty wine bottles lying around, too. The sheriff's officers decided that a theft ring was probably taking stolen bikes out there, taking the good parts off of them and leaving the rest. While the thieves worked, they partied on wine.

We would come across cars occasionally that had gotten stuck in the sand, and their owners had just walked away and left them. Some of them had been out there for years.

I'd recommend the Border Patrol to any young person looking for a career job, but today the young P.A.s – *Patrol Agents*, they changed the titles a few years ago – tell me that the patrol has changed, and I wouldn't like it so much now. When we were on a chase, we'd stay on it until it was too dark to see, and then we'd be back out there at first light the next morning and stay on the trail until we caught the aliens. Now, I'm told, at the end of the shift, they break off the chase and go home. I wouldn't like that.

John Evangelist retired from the Border Patrol on December 31, 1977. After retirement he remained in El Centro where he was an athletic trainer at Central and Southwest high schools for many years. He passed away on August 18, 2002.

The foregoing was excised and edited from an autobiography dictated by John Evangelist and transcribed by Anastasia Vellas in July of 1991. It appears here by the courtesy of John's widow, Mrs. Pauline Evangelist.

\+ + + + + + +

KEEP OUT!

by

Tim Waller

Raymond Lazarski and I first met back in the early seventies at supervisors' school after we had both been promoted to Senior Patrol Inspector at Eagle Pass, Texas, and we became personal friends as well as colleagues. *Ski* had been stationed in Eagle Pass for some time before he made Senior; his wife, Lucha, was a local girl, and *Ski* was acquainted with a lot of people and knew his way around in Eagle Pass as well as in Piedras Negras, across the line in Mexico. He was a good friend to have at that time.

On the day of the incident, Ray and Lucha had invited my wife, Karen and I to go with them to a dinner dance at a restaurant in Piedras Negras. It was sort of a formal affair, and the ladies got all *gussied up* in their long dresses. *Ski* and I dressed in our suits, white shirts, and neckties, which were usually reserved for funerals and weddings.

Later in the evening, the party slowed down a bit, and *Ski* suggested that the four of us take a walk outside; there was something on the patio that he wanted us to see. We followed him out onto the patio and until we came to a locked gate with fairly large *KEEP OUT* sign permanently attached. Well, what can I say? I suppose that we all had partied just long enough by then that a locked gate and *keep out* sign was just too much of a temptation to resist. Besides, we were in Mexico; if they really meant for us to stay out, the sign would have been in Spanish. Makes sense, doesn't it?

Ski fiddled with the lock on the gate for a minute, and the darn thing just fell off. Imagine that? Must have been a cheap lock.

We followed *Ski* through the gate and into a compound where there were several large cages constructed of heavy chain link fence, and inside the cages there were several black bears. The bears seemed to be docile, and we stood there and watched them pace back and forth in the cages for a few minutes. Then someone – I don't remember now who it was – noticed that the bears' watering troughs were dry. Good Samaritans that we all were, we opened the faucet to fill the troughs with water, thinking all the time, of course, that the bears would be most appreciative of our good deed. But bears tend to be testy and unpredictable.

Suddenly, the biggest of the bears – he must have weighed three hundred pounds – let out a mighty roar and charged at the chain link fence separating us from the animals. He seemed to be awful mad about something. He kept growling and snorting, and he got his head, his neck, and his front paws under the fence. I thought that he was going to come right on through and eat me alive.

My hair stood on end. I back-peddled about ten feet, and I turned around hollering something about getting the hell out of there. I might as well have saved my breath; the others were already well ahead of me. The girls were leading the way, running full-out with their long skirts gathered up in their hands.

Fortunately, the monster bear didn't get all the way through the chain link fence, and we escaped without a scratch. Thinking back on it now, we laugh about our encounter with the rowdy and unappreciative bear,.... but we have a lot more respect for *keep out* signs.

\+ \+ \+ \+ \+ \+ \+

Involuntarily Transferred to U. S. Customs

by

Wes Selman

I believe that it was about 1958; I was working the Greyhound Bus station in San Diego, California, with Julian Shefstad. John "Red" Foquette was the supervisor.

The bus station in San Diego in those days occupied about a third of the west end of the block between First Street and Front Street, just east of Broadway. There was another building – I don't remember what it was – that occupied about a third of the block on the east end, and the space between was used to park out-of-service busses. Directly across First Street on the north was the San Diego County Jail. That particular night, there was a row of busses parked close to the building along the east side of the bus station.

Julian and I had just arrived to start the shift, and we were talking to Red just outside the little *office* that the bus station management provided for us. I use the term *office* loosely; it was actually the lost baggage storage room, but they let us keep a desk and a trash can in there, and we used it to interrogate aliens when we needed to get out of the public view. We didn't spend any more time in there than absolutely necessary. As we were talking, we noticed a man running across First Street toward the bus station. As he crossed the street, his hat flew off, but he didn't seem to notice, and he didn't make any effort to retrieve it. When he got to the bus parking lot, he ran between the row of parked busses and the building, as though he was trying to hide. Red said, "Something's wrong there; get that guy!"

Julian ran behind the busses, and I ran toward Front Street, planning to *cut him off at the pass*, so to speak. Just as I reached the sidewalk on Front Street, he came out from behind the busses and ran toward Broadway, with me on his heels. I yelled at him to *stop* in English and Spanish, and I may have used a choice expletive or two, but he paid no attention to me.

Finally, I caught up to the running man, timed my steps, and tripped him up. When he fell into the gutter, I grabbed one of his arms and tried to put a hammer lock on him, but he was a little bigger that me, scared, and full of adrenalin. Try as I might, I couldn't hold him down, and we were dancing around in a circle when Julian came up behind us and grabbed his other arm. We got handcuffs on him, and we marched him back to our *office*. On the walk back, he was mumbling something about hitting someone, but neither of us could understand what he was trying to say. We were all out-of-breath and panting by that time.

Red suggested that we take him over to the county jail. Of course, by that time we all suspected that he might be an escapee, so we marched him across the street and into the courtyard where prisoners were taken into the jail.

It didn't take long to identify him. A Deputy U.S. Marshal had been bringing some federal prisoners back to the jail from court, and our man had been among them. He was a marijuana smuggler, and he had just that afternoon been sentenced to five years in prison. He apparently didn't think much of the idea of spending the next five years behind bars.

The prisoners had been handcuffed together in the back of the marshal's van, but our man had somehow managed to slip his wrist out of the handcuff that connected him to another prisoner. When the deputy marshal opened the back door of the van, our man slammed the door into him, knocking him down. Then our man took off toward the bus station and the man who had been handcuffed to him took off in the opposite direction. Sheriff's deputies caught the other man almost immediately, but there weren't enough officers on the scene to go chasing after our man.

There were already newspaper reporters on the scene at the county jail when we got there. Red gave the reporters the facts and our names, and he stressed that we were U.S. Border Patrol officers. The next morning, the whole story came out in the newspaper; our names weren't mentioned and we were identified as U.S. Customs agents.

\+ + + + + + +

Border Patrol Airline
by

Ed Woods

Looking back in my dusty old log books brings to mind an incident that occurred in the late sixties. I was flying the airlift then. Bill Kane, Roy Beathard, and I had the old Border Patrol DC-4, tail number N1866C; I'll never forget that number.

It was supposed to be a two trip day, El Paso to El Centro and back, and then do it again. It was August, and we made the first round-trip in the cool of the morning, and everything went fine. As the day progressed the temperature climbed -- it does that in the Southwest desert in August, you know -- and by the time we got back to El Centro on the second trip the heat waves rising from the runway at the Naval Air Station looked like a shimmering mirage. The temperature on the ramp where we had to park the airplane in the middle of acres of concrete must have been close to a hundred thirty-five degrees in the shade, and, of course, there wasn't any shade.

We loaded up a hundred illegal aliens – by the way, they were *illegal* in those days, not *undocumented*

– closed the door, fired-up all four engines, and taxied out to the end of the runway. At the end of the runway, we ran-up all of the engines, which was normal procedure, and number two decided to burp and belch. So we taxied back to the ramp so the mechanic could check out the engine and hopefully fix whatever might be wrong.

While the mechanic worked on the engine, we unloaded the illegal aliens and loaded them back on the busses that had brought them to the Naval Air Station from the detention facility. The temperature inside the busses continued to rise as we waited for the mechanic to finish his work, and our *cargo* continued to ripen. Some of those fellers hadn't had a bath in a while.

Finally, the mechanic finished, we loaded our somewhat less than happy travelers aboard, and taxied to the end of the runway again. No go this time, either; we were still burping and belching.

We started back to the ramp, and a smart-ass in the control tower says, "Six-Six Charlie, what do you want now?" in a sarcastic voice. Roy Beathard, an ex-Navy airplane driver, wasn't impressed, and he said, "We're goin' back to the ramp! So what?" He said it in a voice that invited no further discussion, and there was not another word from the tower.

Off again and into the busses with the aliens, who were not only ripe but getting a little grumpy by now, as was the crew of Six-Six Charlie.

While the mechanic worked on the engine, I stood under the wing in the shade watching him. It wasn't cool, but it was a damn site cooler than inside that airplane. I spotted a horny toad running around frantically on the ramp with a stick in his mouth trying to jab the end of it into the concrete. When I asked the mechanic what the varmint thought he was doing, he replied, "He's tryin' to stick that stick in the ground so he can crawl up on it and cool his feet." I might have known. I didn't ask any more questions.

About an hour later, the mechanic has number two fixed, he says. We load up the aliens again; man they were really stinkin' now, and they didn't seem too anxious to get into that hot airplane. I saw several of them crossing themselves, and I heard the Spanish version of *Hail Mary* a number of times. Nevertheless, they all got aboard and we got the door closed.

This time we got through the run-up in good order, and we blasted off for El Paso, or so we thought.

We had just gotten off the ground and started to raise the landing gear when all hell broke loose: A loud bell started ringing and red light came on on the instrument panel. "Zone one fire! Number four engine," I yelled at the top of my voice.

Bill hollers to Roy, "Is it burning?"

Roy calmly looks out the window and says in his calm voice, as though he were announcing that dinner is served, "Yep, Bill. She's a burnin'."

Bill orders, "Feather number four!"

I hit the feather button, mixture and prop, and I feel something running down between my shoulder blades, sweat. Sure, it's sweat. It's still hot inside the airplane; who wouldn't be sweating. That's my story and I'm stickin' to it.

Just then the control tower comes on the radio and says, "Six-Six Clarlie, you've got an engine fire in number four." Bill tells them that we're coming back again. No smart-ass comments from the controller this time.

After we land and taxi back to the ramp, I

looked back into the cabin: a hundred Mexicans all making the sign of the cross and mumbling *Hail Maria, madre de Dios...*" When we opened the door, they ran for the safety of the busses.

After dark that night, Bill, Roy, and I flew back to El Paso on three engines without our passengers. Just after we lifted off in El Centro, the smart-ass in the control tower said, "I hope you fellers had a nice day." We ignored him, it just wasn't worth the effort.

When I got home that night, Ma gave me a big hug, and I told her it was true: Multiengine flying was hour upon hour of boredom interrupted by moments of sheer terror.

That was not to be my longest trip on three engines. Later on, I flew from Atlanta, Georgia, to Brownsville, Texas, with number two prop stored in the baggage compartment.

The airlift was inaugurated in 1954, and in 1970 the pilots at El Paso were honored with an award for fifteen years, seventy-one thousand pilots hours, and 290 million passenger miles, which included many overseas flights to Europe, without a fatality. That was no small accomplishment taking into account that it was all done with surplus military aircraft.

When the awards were to be presented, they had us all dressed up and lined up for a picture, but there was to be no group picture. They said that there was no film in the camera. Truth be told, one of the pilots probably broke the damn thing. *Que lastima, hombres!*

\+ + + + + + +

The Salt and Pepper Tag Team

by

Bob Stille

It must have been around 1985, I believe. It was a Sunday afternoon, and I was Patrol Agent in Charge at Campo, California. I had gone to the Port of Entry at Tecate that afternoon to talk to the Inspectors about something; I can't remember exactly what it was, but it was business. I was in the office talking to the INS supervisor when suddenly one of the Immigration Inspectors, Elaine Campbell, in a booth on a vehicle lane started hollering for help. She sounded desperate, and Customs Inspector John Sullivan and I rushed out to see what was going on.

A good-sized Mexican man was in the booth with Elaine babbling, half in English and half in Spanish, in a threatening manner. I grabbed the guy by the arm and yanked him out of the booth, where he didn't belong in the first place. Elaine immediately abandoned ship and ran into the safety of the office, leaving John and I to deal with the man. That was sound judgment on her part, as the man was obviously violent and out of control, and she would just have been in the way while John and I were trying to subdue him had she remained.

The man appeared to be about forty-five years old, and he was clean and well-dressed. He wore a trendy sport shirt unbuttoned down to his stomach, and he had a gold chain around his neck from which hung a large jewel encrusted gold pendant. He didn't appear to be on welfare.

As I struggled with the man, he was ranting something about *little men* being after him, and he was stomping the pavement with his feet as though he were stomping on ants or possibly something a little bit bigger. He was strong as a bull, and he was a real handful. He and I danced around for a minute, and then he jerked loose from me, went into a classic martial arts stance, and told me in English that he was a *black belt.*

All of this was going on in the traffic lane in front of a car waiting for inspection, and when the man started to make a move on me, I grabbed him in a bear hug, swung him around, and pushed him across the hood of the waiting automobile. A Mexican man and a woman in the front seat of the car were watching with eyes as big as saucers.

I put my entire six foot five and two hundred eighty-five pound frame on him, and I held him down while John Sullivan got my handcuffs off my belt and tried to handcuff him. The guy was so strong that I had a difficult time just getting his arms behind his back so that John could get the handcuffs on his wrists, but we finally got him handcuffed.

About this time, Patrol Agent Greg Ward arrived on the scene and came over to see if he could help. Greg is a black guy, almost as big as I am, and ordinarily easy going. Now that we had the man handcuffed with his hands behind his back, I thought that we had him under control, and I let him get to his feet. That was a mistake; he wasn't finished fighting.

The man had no more than regained his feet when he started kicking out, as martial arts students are taught to do, and he landed one of his kicks square into Greg Ward's groin. As you can imagine, that didn't please Greg a great deal, and he landed a solid punch which sent the man sprawling on his back on the ground. We rolled him over, took off his belt, and hogtied him with it. Then we carried him into the office like a sack of potatoes and put him in the customs lockup.

Customs officers took over at that point. They tried to question him, but all they got out of him was nonsensical babble, half in English and half in Spanish. He kept hollering that *little men* were after him. He had no identification, and no one there at the time recognized him. The Customs officers decided to call the Mexican police in an effort to find out who he was and what he was up to.

A Tecate, Baja California, police *sargento* came over to see if he could help, but he didn't have any more luck with the man than we were having. As the man appeared to be Mexican, and he hadn't technically entered the United States, it was decided that the Mexican *sargento* would take him back to Mexico. We carried the guy out, still hogtied and still kicking and fighting, and put him facedown in the back seat of the Mexican police car. The Mexican policeman promised to bring my handcuffs back to me once he had the man securely in jail. I had known the policeman for some time, and under the circumstances, I decided to trust him with my handcuffs.

About three hours later, the Mexican police *sargento* brought my handcuffs back, and I asked him what they had done with the man. He told me, in his less than perfect English, " You know, when we put him in the cell and take the handcuffs off, he get real angry. He rip the toilet out from the floor and throw it at us. A bunch of us guys had to go in and put him down again. Then he was real sad, and he was crying. So we left him alone and lock the cell door. When we come back to check on him, we find out he hang himself. Now he is dead."

Shortly after the *sargento* departed, a local DEA agent stopped by, and we were telling him about the incident. He wanted to know the guys name. The Customs officers had gotten it from the Mexican policeman, and when they told him, the DEA agent went ballistic. He pulled the FBI wanted bulletins off the wall, and about twenty down in the stack, he found the bulletin that he wanted. There was no mistaking; the picture looked exactly like our man. DEA had been looking for the man for more than a year. There was an arrest warrant outstanding for smuggling tons of marijuana, and his bond had been set at a quarter of a million dollars. He was one of four brothers who lived in Tijuana and were considered among the largest and most active *narco-traficantes* around at that time. The agent jumped into his car and rushed over to Mexico to see what he could find out about what the man was doing in Tecate and how he had died.

The DEA agent got back to me the next day. All that he was able to find out, beyond what we had told him, was that our man was a good friend of a man who owned a large restaurant in Tecate who was also known to be a drug smuggler. Apparently, our man had gotten on the wrong side of some criminals in Mexico, and someone had a put a *hit* out on him. He was on the run, and he apparently had been sampling some of his own merchandise. At the time that he showed up at the Port of Entry, he may have been looking for asylum in the United States, but he was so blasted out of his mind on dope that he couldn't make himself be understood. In any case, it was now a moot point.

The DEA agent also told me that there was a big *stink* in Mexico over the circumstances of the guy's death. It wasn't so much that he was dead or how he had died, but there were a lot of questions being asked about a gold chain and a gold *broach* worth more than thirty thousand dollars that seemed to be missing. I told the agent that he was wearing the chain and the broach around his neck when we put him into the Mexican police car. Where did it go? And who killed him? I don't know the answers to either of these questions, but my money's on the Mexican cops.

Gregg Ward and I took some good-natured ribbing about this incident for quite some time afterward. We are both big guys, and we both had wrestled in college. We were dubbed *The Salt and Pepper Tag Team.*

\+ + + + + + +

The Suggestion Box

by

Norman Howe

For the benefit of those of you who didn't have the pleasure of being there, Presidio, Texas, at the south end of Texas Highway 67, in the early sixties was truly the end of the road. There were no televisions, no movies, no video rentals – we didn't know what a video tape was in those days – and darn few radio programs. There were no night clubs, supermarkets, or malls, either. Entertainment for a P.I. and his family came in the form of welcoming and farewell *pachangas* and creating enduring friendships among the other unfortunates stationed there. Of course, there was also the vast open sky full of stars, the river full of fish, and the mountains full of game, not to mention a few clever minds full of mischief, to make life interesting.

As you might expect, there wasn't a long list of Patrol Inspectors applying for duty in Presidio, Texas, and an officer's transfer there was sometimes precipitated by some premeditated or accidental misadventure somewhere else. Of the twelve of us stationed there in 1960, more than just a few could be described as being both *innovative* and *resourceful* when it came to creating diversions and adding a little spice to life.

Our station at that time was an old army building that had been moved to the site and converted into office space, complete with electricity and indoor plumbing, which made it one of the more modern buildings in town. The building was painted in the official white and green for easy identification, and our two sedans and several rag-top jeeps were parked under the small carport or out back in the parking lot when they weren't in use.

Jack Brunson was the station Senior Patrol Inspector, and there was never a nicer guy or better boss than Jack. Why is it that stuff always happens to the nice guys?

On the day that I'm thinking of, we were scheduled for our annual inspection by the folks from the Central Office in Washington. The office and the vehicles were sparkling clean and polished, the grounds neatly policed, and all hands were in dress greens, brass and leather gleaming, as the inspection party led by the Chief Patrol Inspector from Marfa – I believe it was Chief Smith at the time, another nice guy – arrived. I don't remember a lot about what took place for the greater part of that day, but I clearly remember how it ended.

Nailed to the wall at about shoulder height in the squad room was a little box; I believe that it had started life as a cigar box, but it had been outfitted with a hinged lid on top, painted white, and the word *SUGGESTIONS* printed in black neatly across its middle. We all knew that the box was there; we saw it every day, but nobody ever paid much attention to it.

One of the Central Office inspectors noticed the suggestion box hanging on the wall, and he asked Jack if it was being used. Jack's reply was something to the effect that the suggestion box was an important part of the station's operation, and that he checked its contents periodically. The inspector reached into the box and extracted one folded, yellowing, and dusty piece of paper. He carefully opened the note, read it, and then handed it to Jack. The note, scribbled out in pencil on an official suggestion form and signed by some long ago and forgotten horse riding P.I.:

> *I think that it might be a good idea to trade in some of our Model A's for the new, more powerful Hudson Terraplanes. They're fast, and they can pull a horse trailer on the gravel roads that now stretch for miles up and down the river. This would cut down on our feed bill, water, and saddle sore butts, as well.*

Jack's face colored, but nobody said a word, and then Jack, the chief, and the inspectors disappeared into Jack's office and closed the door. A few minutes later, the chief and the inspectors reappeared, jumped into their cars, and drove away without a word to any of us. So that ended the matter,....well,....not quite.

About two weeks later, Jack got a memo advising him that the suggestion form used by the *old P.I.* was a 1957 revision. Therefore, the bogus suggestion was obviously perpetrated by some malcontent in the Presidio station, who should be uncovered and dealt with harshly.

The culprit was never discovered, and the whole incident was quietly forgotten, by everyone but Jack Brunson, that is. Every few days Jack would reach into the little box and check for any suggestions that might have been deposited therein. Of course, he never found any, but he continued to look, especially on those days when the chief of some other government official was to visit the station.

Several weeks after the first incident, the chief was due to visit, and Jack, as had become his custom, stuck his hand into the suggestion box to make sure that there wasn't anything embarrassing there. He jerked his hand back and yelped as the mouse trap snapped shut on his finger. After that, the suggestion box was permanently removed, the holes in the wall patched with plaster, and the site painted over.

Jack Brunson was one of those rare individuals who never lost his temper and who seemed always to be in complete control, but we all knew that he was teetering on the edge this time. We agreed that neither the incident nor the suggestion box should ever be mentioned again,... and it never has been,... until now.

\+ \+ \+ \+ \+ \+

John Harris Behan

A Man Much Maligned

by

Gene Botts

Western fiction writers and so-called local historians, usually self-appointed and self-anointed, have made popular heroes of some of the darnedest characters who ever stumbled across the Old West. This is especially true in the borderlands of the Southwest. Wyatt Earp is a good example.

At least two dozen books have been written glorifying Wyatt Earp and expounding upon his heroics as a frontier lawman. Hollywood has made no less than five full-length motion pictures based upon the heroic exploits of *Marshal Wyatt Earp* and *The Gunfight at the O.K. Corral*, and he has been given smaller but equally heroic parts in dozens of other films. *The Legend of Wyatt Earp*, a series of one-hour weekly episodes appeared on network television for several years running, and the show had a large following in the United States and many foreign countries as well.

Tombstone, Arizona, has become an unholy tourist trap like no other in the world, and it's all based upon the *legend* of Wyatt Earp. Everything imaginable is for sale there with Wyatt Earp's name or image emblazoned on it. For a rather substantial price of admission, you can see local actors reenact the shooting at the O.K. Corral, *just as it happened and where it happened on October 26, 1881.* Well,... maybe not *exactly* where it happened, but pretty close. And it's not portrayed *exactly* as it happened, but the way they tell it today makes the Earps look better and sells more tickets and more souvenirs.

This is all harmless fun, of course, and quite a few people are making a living spinning yarns, playacting, and selling Old West memorabilia. There's one little problem with all of this Wyatt Earp hero-worship, though; it's not exactly the *gospel* truth. I'm not so sure that there is a *hero* in the Tombstone story, but if there has to be a hero, Sheriff John Harris Behan comes closer than anyone else.

When the storytellers and the moviemakers bother to mention John Behan at all, he is consistently portrayed as inept, crooked, and a whimpering coward. In their zeal to create the bigger-than-life Marshal Wyatt Earp, the pseudo historians and the western fiction writers have carelessly libeled and slandered a man who was an honest, competent, and legitimate lawman for many years before and after the famous gunfight in Tombstone.

John Behan was a courageous Arizona pioneer, and he was an honorable man. He was also one of the first federal officers to patrol the Mexican border enforcing United States customs and immigration laws. He has been unfairly maligned for more than seventy years in order to enhance the false image of Wyatt Earp and his brothers, and it's time that the record is set straight.

Wyatt Earp was never, ever the town marshal in Tombstone, Arizona, or anywhere else, so far as I've been able to determine, and I've spent a considerable amount of time looking into his background. He was a few times a *deputy* town marshal, but never for any extended period of time. It is true that he was a *constable* in Lamar, Missouri, for a while in 1869 – his father was the Justice of the Peace – but he only served a few weeks before he left town in a hurry, something about a stolen horse.

In Wichita and Dodge City, Kansas, where Wyatt Earp was supposed to have made his early reputation as a relentless lawman, he was probably a rent-a-cop. The saloons in those trailhead towns were a combination of drinking establishment, gambling hall, and whorehouse under one roof, and they catered to a rough crowd. The owners found it to be to their mutual benefit to form an association and hire their own policemen. The so-called *Dodge City Peace Commission* and its counterpart in Wichita were not city police forces as we know them today. Wyatt Earp and his cohorts were for the most part a gang of toughs and gunslingers hired by the saloon owners to keep the peace and protect their employers' property. They were basically saloon bouncers. To be charitable, we might call them *security officers* today. A few of them would later become legitimate lawmen, but Wyatt Earp's claim to have been among the few is shaky at best.

Although the saloon owners hired and paid the private policemen, they were nominally appointed deputies of the town marshal to give them an appearance of respectability. The town marshal was supposed to supervise them, but in reality he had little influence over their hiring or their behavior on the job. There is a rumor, however, that the town marshal in Dodge City so disapproved of Wyatt Earp's heavy-handed methods that he was instrumental in having Earp fired.

Wyatt Earp's major source of income throughout most of his life was from gambling, promoting horse races and boxing matches, and speculating in mining ventures and real estate. His name and his brothers' names appear on a dozen or more early Arizona titles and mining claims, but there is no evidence to suggest that any of the Earps ever swung a pick or pushed a shovel in a mine. The Earps were not fond of hard work, and it's a good guess that the money for all of these investments came from gambling.

Of the six Earp brothers, only Virgil was a legitimate lawman. Before he went to Tombstone, Virgil was the town marshal in Prescott, Arizona Territory. He was a big man, not overly bright, but good-natured and even tempered. He was basically honest, friendly to a fault, and well liked. His size and his even temperament made it rarely necessary for him to resort to violence to enforce the laws and keep the peace. When physical force did become necessary, it was usually his big hands and a booted foot that got the job done. Virgil hardly ever found it necessary to use a firearm. From all accounts, Virgil did a good job as town marshal in Prescott. He should have stayed there.

The seat of the Arizona territorial government was in Prescott, and Virgil was a close friend of Crawley Dake, the United States Marshal for the territory. Crawley Dake, was a well-educated man, a Union Army major during the Civil War, and he had been treasurer of the State of Michigan before he went to Arizona. He was also a consummate politician with considerable political influence in Washington, and he was arrogant beyond words of description.

As United States Marshal in Arizona, Crawley Dake seems to have suffered from the same problems that so plagued the United States Border Patrol for so many years: he was constantly and continually short of operating funds. He needed a lot of help to cover his vast territory, but the Attorney General in Washington continually ignored his repeated requests for funding and failed to provide money for him to pay the salaries of a sufficient number of regular deputy marshals.

In order to accomplish the mission of his office, Crawley Dake appointed a number of *special deputies* who he paid for each assignment from the same register of fees that he used for his regular deputies; although, he did not have the authority to do so. Of course, all of these *special* deputies had to have other sources of income to sustain themselves and their families.

When Virgil Earp decided to move to Tombstone Crawley Dake did not have a deputy there, so he appointed Virgil a *special* deputy U. S. Marshal. The appointment carried with it no salary, but it would give Virgil a few extra dollars in fees occasionally and a certain status in his new community. His duties as a deputy federal marshal wouldn't take much of his time.

Unlike in the Oklahoma Territory and a few other places in the early days of the West, civil authority never broke down in the Arizona Territory to the extent that it was necessary to introduce federal officers to restore order.

Contrary to what western fiction writers and

Hollywood would have us believe, federal marshals had very limited authority even in the territories, and they didn't ordinarily involve themselves in day to day local law enforcement any more than they do today. Most everything that the federal marshals did was done under a court order, no court order, no authority.

Federal marshals enforced only a few federal criminal laws in the early days. They had statutory authority to protect the mails, and on the basis of that authority they investigated stagecoach and train robberies. Most crimes of the day were in the jurisdiction of the local sheriffs, and the local establishment in the Arizona Territory was very jealous of its jurisdiction and authority.

Who had the authority to do what, where, and when did sometimes get confusing. Many of the deputy federal marshals carried two badges, a federal badge and a local badge concurrently, which certainly added to the confusion. And a few of them did on occasion exceed their authority for personal and political reasons. They were seen as federal officers, and most people didn't understand the limitations of their authority. Some of them got way out-of-line. The newspapers of the day are full of stories about federal marshals *overstepping their bounds*.

When Virgil Earp arrived in Tombstone with his deputy federal marshal badge and a letter of introduction from Crawley Dake, he went directly to see John P. Clum, the publisher of the *Tombstone Epitaph* and the acknowledged leader of Republican politics in the vicinity.

Virgil needed a job, and John Clum arranged for him to be appointed a deputy town marshal. A few weeks later, when the town marshal was accidentally shot and killed trying to disarm a drunken cowboy, he was appointed temporary town marshal to serve until the next regular election.

The businessmen in Tombstone, the merchants, the gamblers, and the mine operators, mostly associated themselves with the Republican party, while the farmers and the ranchers and the cowboys living in the surrounding area were mostly Democrats. The Democrats were probably in the majority, as they were in most of Southern Arizona after the Civil War, but there was little doubt as to who held the political power in Tombstone, and the Earp brothers quickly associated themselves with John Clum and the Republicans.

There were five Earp brothers in Tombstone in its heyday, James, Morgan, Warren, Wyatt, and Virgil. There was another half-brother in the family, Newton, but so far as I've been able to determine, he never made it to Arizona.

James and Warren seemed content to keep a low profile. James had been seriously wounded in the Civil War, and he had never fully recovered. He was slightly handicapped, worked as a bartender, and minded his own business.

Warren also busied himself with his own affairs, and he stayed out of trouble, at least in the beginning. After the affair at the O.K. Corral, when the rest of the Earps left the territory, Warren stayed behind. A few years later he managed to get himself killed in a gunfight in a Willcox saloon, but that's another story.

Wyatt busied himself with his gambling concession in one of the saloons and his part-time job as a Wells-Fargo guard until John Clum suggested to him that he become a deputy sheriff. John Clum knew that Pima County Sheriff Charles Shibell in Tucson was looking for a man to be his resident deputy in Tombstone. Everyone was aware that the territorial legislature would soon create Cochise County from the eastern portion of Pima County, and Tombstone would become the county seat. The Republican governor, General John C. Fremont, would appoint the first officers of the new county to serve until the next general elections. John Clum theorized that if Wyatt were the deputy sheriff in Tombstone at the time the new county was created, he would stand an excellent chance of being appointed sheriff.

Wyatt turned his Wells-Fargo job over to his brother, Morgan, and he applied for the deputy sheriff position, probably greatly exaggerating his experience as a lawman in Dodge City and Wichita. Although Wyatt was generally closemouthed, even to the point of rudeness on occasion, he could be a glib and persuasive talker when he wanted to be, and he convinced the sheriff to hire him. However, he didn't hold the position for very long. He resigned, probably by request, three months later.

Democrats said that the sheriff had been getting complaints from Tombstone residents about Wyatt's brutal methods in dealing with minor offenders. He had a nasty habit of beating drunks over the head with the barrel of his six-shooter to subdue them. He called the practice *buffaloing* them, a term he probably picked up from the thugs he worked with in Dodge City and Wichita. Republicans said that Sheriff Shibell wanted rid of Wyatt because he had been openly campaigning for Shibell's rival in the coming election. There are ample grounds to believe that both stories are true.

Wyatt returned to gambling, promoting horse

races and sporting events, and occasionally helping his brother as an unpaid deputy town marshal. All of the town marshals had been elected or appointed by the town council, and there were no provisions in the law or the town charter for town marshals to appoint their own deputies, but that minor legality didn't seem to impede the Earp brothers.

In the long run, Wyatt's help may not have been of great benefit to Virgil's career. When the next election came around, Virgil put his name on the ballot expecting to easily win, but a drifter named Ben Sippy, who had only been in town a few weeks and hardly knew anyone, defeated him. It's possible that the way his brothers, Wyatt and Morgan, had been helping Virgil keep the peace may have contributed to his defeat at the polls. As it turned out, however, this was only a small bump in the road. Ben Sippy soon gave up the job for no apparent reason and left town. Virgil was once again appointed temporary town marshal.

John Harris Behan was born in 1845, in Missouri, one of nine children of Irish immigrant parents who saw to it that he and his siblings got at least the rudiments of a decent education.

When John was seventeen years old in 1862, he left home alone and found his way to San Francisco. With little money and no immediate prospects for a job, he joined the Union Army. Later that same year, he marched into the Arizona Territory with the California Column sent to drive the Confederate troops then encamped in Tucson out of the territory. He may have participated in the battle at Picacho Peak, the only Civil War battle fought in Arizona. He seems to have been at the right place at the right time, but I haven't been able to confirm that he took part in the fighting. It makes little difference to our story, anyway. The battle only lasted a few minutes before the Confederates withdrew. By the time the Yankee force reached Tucson, the Confederates had packed-up and departed.

John Behan was released from the Army in 1865 in Prescott, and he decided to stay there. Prescott was a crude, rough, and inhospitable town at the time, as was the whole of the territory, but it presented opportunities for an ambitious young man. He didn't have a lot of money or higher education to recommend him, but he was a hard worker, smart, and determined. He took any job he could get in the early days, saved his money, and invested in a number of small business ventures, mining, freighting, anything to make a few dollars honestly. He soon became well-known and respected in the community, and he began to involve himself in Democratic politics.

John married Victoria Zaff in the spring of 1869, and they had two children, Henrietta in 1869 and Albert in 1871. Their daughter died of an illness in 1874, and their marriage began to sour soon afterward. It ended in 1875 when Victoria filed a petition for divorce on grounds that John was consorting with a prostitute named *Sada*.

It may or may not have been true that John was consorting with a prostitute; divorces were very difficult to get in territorial Arizona, and fictitious liaisons were often alleged and admitted merely to obtain a divorce when both parties wanted to end the marriage. It was customary and considered gentlemanly for a man to allow his wife to file the petition for divorce in order to save her from ridicule and embarrassment. At this late date, no one will ever know for sure if John Behan was actually consorting with a prostitute named *Sada.* It's certainly possible; everywhere he lived for most of his life, John acquired a reputation with the ladies. It makes little difference now, but many of his political rivals during his lifetime as well as many writers in later years have used his reputation and the wording of Victoria's petition for divorce to assault his character.

Young Albert continued to live with his mother after the divorce was granted, but when she remarried four years later, he went to live with his father.

John Behan became a deputy sheriff in Yavapai County in 1867, but he resigned early in 1868 when he was elected county recorder. He held that job until 1871, when he was elected sheriff of Yavapai County. In 1873, he was elected a representative to the territorial legislature from Yavapai County. Then in 1878, he moved to neighboring Mojave County and ran for sheriff. He lost that election, but he was immediately hired as a deputy by the man who he had opposed in the election. Later the same year he was elected to a Mojave County seat in the territorial legislature. He continued to serve as a deputy sheriff for several years, but he was also involved in several small businesses in both Yavapai and Mojave counties at the same time.

When it became apparent to politicians of both parties that the legislature was about to create Cochise County, John was encouraged by his Democratic friends in Prescott to relocate to Tombstone and seek the county sheriff position when the new county was established. They reasoned that if he couldn't get the initial appointment from the Republican governor, he could run for the office at the next general election. They calculated that the population of what would be the new county was almost equally divided between Republicans and Democrats, and they believed that John's record of achievement in both business and politics and his experience as a lawman would give the Democrats the edge in the election.

In the fall of 1879, John and nine-year-old Albert moved to Tombstone. He bought a house in town and immediately invested in a livery stable with Thomas Dunbar, a fellow Democrat who was at the time Tombstone's representative to the territorial legislature.

Shortly after John Behan arrived in Tombstone, Josephine (Josey) Marcus, the eighteen-year-old runaway daughter of a wealthy San Francisco merchant, arrived with a traveling stage production of the Gilbert and Sullivan operetta *HMS Pinafore.* Ironically, Josephine, who was quite a beautiful and well-developed young lady, played the part of the cabin boy, Tommy Tucker, in male costume.

Just where and when John Behan and Josey Marcus first met has been argued for many years. Some sources claim that they first met on the street in Tombstone. Others say that they knew each other and were lovers in Prescott before John went to Tombstone, and that Josey went to Tombstone expecting John to marry her. Still others say that they met years earlier in San Francisco, which is unlikely, as she would have been an infant at the time he was in San Francisco. Some writers have even claimed that she was the notorious *Sada* mentioned in Victoria's petition for divorce. I think that's unlikely, but it may account for some writers referring to her as *Sadie* Marcus. There is no evidence that she ever used that name.

It's not important when or under what

circumstances John Behan and Josephine Marcus first met. The fact is; she moved into John's home the same day that she arrived in Tombstone. She soon abandoned her acting career and busied herself keeping house for John and looking after young Albert while John pursued his business and political affairs. It's rumored that they were lovers, and given John Behan's reputation as a ladies-man for most of his life and Josephine's untamed nature at the time, it's quite possible that they were lovers. I don't know, and no one else knows.

It was shortly after John Behan's arrival in Tombstone that Wyatt Earp lost his job as deputy sheriff. Sheriff Shibell was a leading Democratic politician in the territory, and he knew John Behan personally from his days in the territorial legislature. He knew that John was living in Tombstone, and he probably knew why he was there. He immediately appointed John to be Tombstone's deputy sheriff in place of Wyatt Earp.

Of course, everyone in the vicinity knew that both Wyatt Earp and John Behan were candidates for the office of sheriff of the new county. John Clum and most of the business community in Tombstone supported Wyatt Earp openly, while John Behan got his support from the cattlemen and settlers in the surrounding area. On the basis of qualifications and experience, John Behan would be the obvious choice. He was known throughout the whole territory, and he had the endorsement of *The Arizona Miner*, the largest and most influential newspaper in the territory at the time:

> ***It seems evident that the new county of Cochise will soon be formed, and in this connection The Miner would respectfully request that John H. Behan be appointed the first sheriff of what is to be one of the most important counties in the territory. He has been tried in this county as sheriff and never found wanting.***
>
> ***The Arizona Miner* - Prescott, A.T. - January 1881**

By contrast, Wyatt Earp was virtually unknown outside of Tombstone, and he had few verifiable credentials for the job.

There was simply no comparison between the qualifications of the two candidates, but Governor Fremont would make the decision. The governor was a long time Republican; however, he was known to be somewhat of an independent maverick in the party since he lost the Republican nomination for president a few years earlier, and the Republican candidate was not necessarily assured of the appointment.

When Wyatt Earp lost his job as deputy sheriff, the Earps and John Clum were understandably upset. They spread a rumor that Wyatt's termination was politically motivated to enhance John Behan's chances of being appointed sheriff in the new county. Although it very well may have been true, the Earps complaints and Clum's editorials weren't taken seriously by many people. A lot of folks had noticed and disapproved of Wyatt Earp's heavy-handed method of law enforcement.

Rumors of *bad blood* between John Behan and Wyatt Earp began to circulate, and to add to the rumors, Josephine Marcus began seeing Wyatt socially while

John was away from home on business. In the fall of 1880, she moved out of John's house and moved into a rented house provided for her by Wyatt Earp.

Wyatt continued living with Mattie (Blaylock) in another house that he owned a few blocks away. Wyatt and Mattie claimed to be married, but it's unlikely that they were ever legally married. They were obviously not getting along at the time. Mattie was a prostitute addicted to Laudanum, a highly addictive preparation of Opium sold openly in those days.

Of course, rumors of Wyatt's having stolen John's woman circulated about town, and writers and *historians* for more than a hundred years have repeated the rumors as though they were gospel. Perhaps there is some kernel of truth in the rumors, but Josey's taking up with Wyatt didn't seem to cause any particular animosity between her and John Behan at the time. They continued to be friends, and she continued to care for Albert when John was away from home for days at a time until the summer of 1882 when she left town to follow Wyatt to California.

In January of 1881, resisting all of the pressures from within his own party, Governor Fremont appointed John Harris Behan to be the first sheriff of Cochise County. John Clum was furious, and he wasn't one to lose gracefully. He made it a practice from then on to criticize the sheriff in almost every issue of the *Tombstone Epitaph*, and John Clum was a master at shading the facts to suit his own ends.

Wyatt Earp didn't give up gracefully, either. He made no secret of the fact that he intended to challenge John Behan in the next election. And in order to establish himself as a lawman and enhance his chances of winning the election, he began meddling in law enforcement affairs whenever the opportunity presented itself, either as Virgil's unpaid and questionably appointed deputy or by claiming to be a Wells-Fargo detective. As to the latter, Wyatt Earp on several occasions claimed to be working for Wells-Fargo as a detective, but according to the Wells-Fargo Museum in San Francisco, he was never employed by that company in any capacity other than as a guard, and then only for a few months.

Wyatt Earp also claimed that John Behan had promised to make him his chief deputy if he were appointed sheriff, and that he had reneged on the promise. Sheriff Behan admitted that he had once approached Wyatt about becoming a deputy in his office should he win the appointment, but changing circumstances had caused him to reconsider and withdraw the offer. It's possible that by the time he became sheriff John was better acquainted with Wyatt Earp's character and deportment, and he changed his mind for that reason.

John Behan was too busy, appointing deputies, organizing his new office, collecting county taxes, and enforcing the law in what was a very large county for a few men to cover on horseback, to be overly concerned about what Wyatt Earp was doing or what the Republicans were saying about him.

Much has been said about the moral character of some of John Behan's deputies, and I'm sure that he later regretted some of his appointments. However, he didn't have a lot to choose from; the mines were in full operation and Tombstone was booming. A miner could make twelve dollars a day, and a bartender could make between four and five dollars a day. Deputy sheriffs were paid two dollars a day. There weren't a lot of men anxious to be deputy sheriffs.

The sheriff's authority, of course, included Tombstone, but John Behan generally left the peace-keeping duties within the town limits to Virgil Earp, who was still the temporary town marshal. Virgil was doing a good job under the circumstances, but it would soon be interrupted by an unfortunate incident that would in later years become known as *the gunfight at the O.K. Corral.*

Over the years since the infamous event at the O.K. Corral, John Behan has been criticized for failing to do his duty on that fateful day. However, even a cursory examination of the *undisputed* facts - most of the facts are *disputed* still today - makes it clear that he did all that could reasonably be expected of him, and he had nothing to apologize for or be ashamed of afterward.

Virgil Earp also did his best that day, and had it not been for the irresponsibility of his brother, Wyatt Earp, there may not have been a shooting at the O.K. Corral. Perhaps, Tombstone today would be a ghost town or just another faded boomtown, and no one would ever have heard of *Marshal Wyatt Earp*.

The trouble that culminated in the shooting began on notorious Allen Street the night before. Ike Clanton was drunk, rowdy, and making a nuisance of himself in the saloons and on the street. The young cowboys who spent most of their lives on the range, tended to *blow-off-steam* on the rare occasions when they went to town. While the gamblers and saloon owners were disposed to overlook rowdy behavior on the part of miners who generally had a pocket full of money to spend, they were not so tolerant of cowboys who had very little money to spend. It wasn't long until

Virgil Earp grabbed Ike and told him to get out of town and sleep it off. Ike decided that he wanted to argue the point, and while he was arguing with Virgil, Wyatt came up behind him and *buffaloed* him.

About noon the following day, someone went to Virgil's house and told him that Ike Clanton was in town, armed, and telling everyone he met that he was *gunning* for the Earps. Virgil then went out to look for Ike, picking up his sawed-off shotgun as he left the house. Before he got very far, he ran into a man named Sills, who claimed to be a railroad engineer who had arrived in town only the day before. Sills supposedly told Virgil that Ike and Billy Clanton, Ike's sixteen-year-old brother, and the McLaury brothers were in the alley behind the O.K. Corral armed and making threats to kill the Earps.

Virgil collected his brothers, Wyatt and Morgan, and they started walking toward the corral, which is located on the west side of town. Somewhere along the way, Doc Holiday, who had been playing poker all night and was probably drunk or hungover, as he was most of the time, joined them. Why Virgil allowed Doc Holiday to accompany them on this mission is a mystery; he had never before involved himself in Virgil's peacekeeping efforts. Doc Holiday was Wyatt's friend, and the record is quite clear that Virgil and the rest of the Earps had no use for the drunken dentist.

Sheriff Behan was in the barbershop on Fremont Street when he saw the Earps and Holiday pass, and he knew something serious was about to happen by the way that they carried themselves. He left the barbershop in a hurry, and caught up to the Earps and Holiday. Virgil told him that they were on their way to the O.K. Corral to disarm the cowboys.

The sheriff personally knew all of the parties involved, and he knew that if there was a confrontation between the Earps and Holiday on the one side and the Clanton brothers and McLaury brothers on the other, someone was going to get hurt. He told Virgil to hold back, and he would go ahead to the O.K. Corral and disarm the cowboys. Virgil agreed, and John Behan ran on ahead.

The sheriff encountered the four cowboys in the alley behind the O.K. Corral. He informed them that they were violating the law by carrying firearms within the town limits, and he had come to disarm them. The cowboys told him that they were armed because they were afraid of the Earps, and they refused to give up their weapons.

While Behan was talking to the cowboys trying to persuade them to give up their weapons or leave town, the Earps and Doc Holiday came up behind him. The sheriff turned toward them and ordered them to stop where they were, but with Virgil in the lead they disregarded the order and approached within a few yards of Sheriff Behan and the cowboys.

Doc Holiday was now carrying Virgil's shotgun. Somewhere along the way, Virgil had given the shotgun to Doc and taken Doc's walking stick. He carried the walking stick in his right hand, his gun hand, and for that reason alone it seems reasonable to assume that Virgil wasn't expecting gunplay. He was probably thinking that he and the sheriff together could defuse the situation without resorting to violence, as they both had done numerous times before.

Why Virgil gave the shotgun to the drunken dentist is another mystery, but it may have been because Doc was a notoriously poor marksman who would have had little chance of surviving a gunfight armed only with a handgun. The legendary Doc Holliday, the hardened gunman and cold-blooded killer, simply isn't true. Doc Holiday wasn't feared in Tombstone; he was looked upon with scorn and contempt for the drunken fool that he was. He was more of a public pest than a menace.

So far as I have been able to determine, John Henry (Doc) Holiday killed no one other than Tom McLaury, who he definitely killed in the gunfight at the O.K. Corral. Whether he actually meant to kill him or he just got overly excited and the shotgun went off by accident is a question that will never be resolved.

When he was drunk and bragging, Doc sometimes claimed to have killed a gambler named Bailey in a dispute over a card game in Fort Griffin, Texas, some years before, but the evidence suggests that it was just *whiskey talk*. There is no record of any such killing, and no grave of the alleged victim in Fort Griffin or anywhere nearby can be found.

Doc may have been involved in some sort of an incident in that town, but at this late date it's not possible to determine with any degree of certainty exactly what happened. It's unlikely that he killed anyone, though. He was run out of town by townspeople who had had quite enough of his drunken, short-tempered, and foulmouthed behavior. If he had killed anyone, I doubt that he would have been let off so lightly.

The often told story of how Wyatt Earp broke him out of jail in Fort Griffin while the townspeople were busy fighting a fire started by Big Nose Kate as a diversion is pure fiction; Doc Holiday did not become acquainted with either of them until much later, and there is no evidence that either Wyatt Earp or Kate Elder were ever in that part of Texas. Besides, Fort Griffin didn't have a jail at that time.

Other than the gunfight at the O.K. Corral, Doc Holiday was involved in only one shooting incident in Tombstone. He had been playing cards in the Oriental Saloon and once again gotten into an altercation with another gambler. He was unarmed at the time, and the saloon owner, Milton Joyce, threw him out. A few minutes later he returned armed with a pistol, a nickel plated Smith and Wesson double action revolver, known at the time as a *self-cocker*. He fired two shots, neither of which came anywhere near his intended victim. One of his bullets hit Milton Joyce in the hand, and the other hit the bartender in the foot. Joyce then whacked Doc over the head with a pistol and turned him over to the town marshal. Doc spent a night in jail and paid a fine for disturbing the peace. The injuries to Milton Joyce and the bartender must have been minor, as no further reference is made to them.

Getting back to the confrontation at the O.K. Corral, according to several witnesses, Virgil Earp raised the walking stick in his right hand and shouted, "Throw up your hands! I have come to disarm you."

One of the cowboys shouted to Sheriff Behan, "We'll give up our guns if you disarm them!" – or words to that effect – pointing toward the Earps and Doc Holiday.

Wyatt Earp then shouted, "You sons-of-bitches! You have been looking for a fight and you can have it."

Both sides drew weapons. Virgil Earp held up

the walking stick and shouted, “Hold on! I don’t mean that!” It was too late; the battle was on.

The fight lasted less than thirty seconds. The witnesses disagree over who fired the first shots, but gunfire was almost simultaneous from both sides. It probably wasn't possible to say who shot first, who shot who, and in what order. It’s clear that Doc Holiday killed Tom McLaury; the effects of the shotgun blast left no doubt, but Tom may have taken one or more bullets from a six-shooter as well.

Virgil switched the walking stick quickly to his left hand, drew his six-shooter, and got off several shots, but he was never sure if he hit anyone.

John Behan quickly took cover in the nearest building, Cyrus Fly's photographic studio, which makes him the only one on the scene to react with any common sense.

Ike Clanton, who it was later determined *was not armed*, approached Wyatt Earp and apparently tried to stop the fight. Wyatt rebuffed him, and he ran down the alley and survived the battle.

When the shooting was over, Billy Clanton and the McLaury brothers were dead. Virgil Earp was wounded in the leg. Doc Holiday and Morgan Earp suffered insignificant flesh wounds. Wyatt Earp didn’t get a scratch.

When the Earps were leaving the scene, Sheriff Behan shouted to Wyatt, “I want to talk to you!”

Wyatt, who was helping the wounded Virgil, replied, “I won’t be arrested now,” and the Earps and Doc Holiday walked away. John Behan let them go.

The *historians* and the fiction writers have told this story in many differing versions. Most of them have concluded that the sheriff was afraid of Wyatt

Earp, and that he was afraid to try to arrest him. I'm inclined to doubt that conclusion; John Behan had previously demonstrated his courage and self-confidence on a number of occasions.

At that particular time, John Behan was the only real law enforcement officer on the scene; Virgil Earp was out of business with a bullet in his leg. He had three homicides to deal with, and a crowd was gathering. The Earps and Doc Holiday were no longer an immediate threat to anyone, and there was no reason to believe that they would be leaving town any time soon. Questioning the Earps and Doc Holiday or arresting anyone could wait; it simply wasn't a priority at the moment. That makes more sense. It's sound judgment, what a well-trained policeman would do in the same circumstances today.

A coroner's inquest followed shortly after the funerals, which resulted in the remarkable conclusion that the deceased had been shot, which was news to no one.

The following day, Ike Clanton filed a criminal complaint before Justice of the Peace Wells Spicer charging the Earps and Doc Holiday with murder. On the basis of that complaint and the sheriff's investigation, arrest warrants were issued for Wyatt Earp and John Henry (Doc) Holiday. Sheriff John Behan didn't hesitate to arrest them both in short order; however, they were each quickly released on $10,000 bail, which they didn't seem to have the least bit of difficulty posting in cash. Warrants were not issued for Virgil and Morgan Earp because of their wounds; although, Morgan's wound was very minor and didn't incapacitate him in the least.

After a preliminary hearing that stretched on for

four weeks before Judge Spicer, a Republican politician and a close personal friend and political ally of John Clum and presumably the Earps, all charges against all parties were dismissed.

The transcript of Judge Spicer's decision is an incredible study of oversight, selective weighing of the evidence, and confused reasoning, but it's quite typical of justice in the American West at the time. The judge held that Wyatt and Morgan Earp and Doc Holiday were duly appointed officers of the law, deputies of the chief of police at the time of the incident - Virgil's title had been changed from town marshal to chief of police by the town council in April of 1881.

Neither Wyatt Earp nor Doc Holiday had ever been appointed policemen in any formal way. On one or two prior occasions, Morgan Earp had been designated a *temporary* policeman, but he was not so commissioned at the time of the incident at the O.K. Corral. There was no legal authority for the town marshal or the chief of police to appoint his own deputies or policemen. The mayor and town council had appointed all previous deputy town marshals and policemen in Tombstone, as was the practice in other towns in the territory. Only the sheriff had legal authority to appoint deputies and raise a posse; although, town marshals and others raised posses to pursue criminals on occasion in other places, such posses had no more authority than private citizens. That point didn't seem to register with Judge Spicer, nor did it seem to matter that the defendants had ignored and disobeyed a lawful order of the county sheriff, the senior law enforcement officer on the scene, to *hold back* and let him handle the cowboys.

No one ever questioned why Virgil Earp had

rounded-up his brothers and Doc Holiday to confront the cowboys in the first place. James Flynn and A.G. Bronk were Tombstone policemen under Virgil's supervision at the time; both had been duly appointed and sworn-in by the town council. Why didn't Virgil Earp call upon them if he needed help to disarm the cowboys? Sheriff Behan was quite obviously willing to take on the task alone.

Judge Spicer seems to have placed greater credibility in the testimony of Mr. H. F. Sills, who claimed to have arrived in town only the day before the shooting, than he did in the testimony of local witnesses; although, he knew nothing of Mr. Sills' character, his background, or his possible motives.

Mr. Sills and his one sided testimony seem to me to be just a little *too* contrived and *too* convenient for the defense. He claimed to be an engineer on the Atchison, Topeka and Santa Fe Railroad, but the A.T. & S.F. tracks pass through Benson, more than twenty miles from Tombstone. What was he doing in Tombstone? And what was he doing hanging around in the alley behind the O.K. Corral so close to the Clantons and the McLaurys that he could overhear their conversation. And where did he go? Immediately after the preliminary hearing, Mr. Sills left town, never to be heard from again. All of the writers and *historians* who have since tried to follow his tracks and identify him have been unsuccessful. Mr. Sills was the surprise witness that defense lawyers dream of but seldom see, and then he disappeared.

Judge Spicer was presiding over a *preliminary hearing* to determine if there was sufficient probable cause to hold the defendants for trial, but he went way beyond the scope of his duty. There was more than sufficient probable cause in the testimony of the witnesses to justify a trial, and there was considerable confusion about the facts and the credibility of the witnesses for a jury to consider. Nevertheless, Judge Spicer let the preliminary hearing drag on for four weeks, and then he dismissed all of the charges against all of the defendants. He wasn't going to let a trial jury get anywhere near this case; they might have convicted the Earps and embarrassed John Clum.

Although they escaped criminal conviction, public sentiment quickly turned against the Earps and Doc Holiday. Virgil Earp was suspended from his job as chief of police, and even John Clum’s *Tombstone Epitaph* backed away from them.

In January of the following year, Virgil was ambushed and shot in the arm as he was walking home on Allen Street one evening. He survived, but he lost the use of his left arm for the rest of his life. The Earps suspected friends of the cowboys killed at the O. K. Corral of the attempt on Virgil's life, but no one has ever been positively identified as the shooter.

Virgil was unable to perform even the limited duties of a part-time deputy U.S. Marshal. Wyatt claimed that he sent a telegram to Crawley Dake asking that he be given Virgil’s relinquished appointment, *with authority to appoint deputies*. Shortly thereafter, Wyatt began wearing Virgil’s badge, and he claimed that Crawley Dake had appointed him a deputy U.S. Marshal and given him the authority to raise a posse. There is no record of any of this in Crawley Dake's papers, and it doesn’t make a lot of sense. I don’t think it was true.

Crawley Dake didn’t know Wyatt Earp personally; they had never met. It’s unlikely that he knew anything about him except hearsay from Virgil and possibly John Clum. Few people outside of Cochise County had ever heard of Wyatt Earp at that time, and it seems unlikely to me that Crawley Dake would have appointed a man he had never met to a position of trust and authority with the added authority *to appoint deputies*, but he may have.

There is no written record of Wyatt Earp ever serving as a deputy U.S. Marshal under Crawley Dake or anyone else. But according to the *Tombstone* Epitaph of February 1, 1882, Crawley Dake visited Tombstone and seems to have acknowledged both Virgil and Wyatt as his deputies. Both Wyatt and Virgil offered their resignations at that time, but Dake refused to accept them. I don't know what his motives were, but I suspect that politics had a lot to do with it.

There is a widely repeated story that Crawley Dake deposited $3,000 into a bank account for Wyatt Earp to draw upon for expenses, but I'm almost sure that story is false. Crawley Dake had seriously overdrawn his government accounts by that time. He had borrowed several thousand dollars in the name of the United States Government, and he was in a dispute with the Treasury Department about unauthorized expenditures totaling several thousand dollars. Bull-headed and arrogant as he was, I still don't think he would have done anything so foolish as to give Wyatt Earp or any other deputy a drawing account in anywhere near that amount.

Crawley Dake's dispute with the Treasury Department seems to have arisen from his appointing and paying his *special* deputies in defiance of regulations, in view of which, Virgil's as well as Wyatt's appointment may have been tainted and illegal.

But all of this happened more than a hundred years ago, and we're a little late to be worrying about it now.

A few weeks after the attempted assassination of Virgil, Morgan was playing pool in Hatch's saloon when a shot came through an open window and shattered his spine. He lived for only about an hour. Again the Earps suspected friends of the cowboys, but again there was no solid evidence. And Morgan was by many accounts a hothead and somewhat of a bully. He kept bad company, and he had more than a few enemies in Tombstone, a number of who were capable of murder.

Marshal Wyatt Earp then raised a posse and went scalp-hunting for the men he suspected were responsible for Virgil's wounding and Morgan's murder. Wyatt's posse consisted of his brother Warren, Doc Holiday, and five or six others of unsavory character, two of whom were suspects in an earlier murder and stagecoach robbery.

Wyatt Earp would have had no legal authority to do any of this even if he were a legitimate deputy U.S. Marshal. No federal warrants had been issued charging anyone with any offense connected with the assault on Virgil and the murder of Morgan. These crimes were strictly within the jurisdiction of the local authorities, Sheriff John Behan and the Tombstone police.

Wyatt Earp's posse never arrested anyone, but according to some accounts he claimed to have killed Florintino Cruz, also known as *Indian Charlie*, at Pete Spence's wood camp in the Dragoon Mountains in what he described as a gunfight; although, it was well-known that Cruz was far less than a skilled gunman. He also claimed to have killed Curly Bill Brocius in a gunfight at Iron Springs in the Whetstone Mountains.

There has been an ongoing dispute among western writers for the past seventy years over Wyatt's claim to have killed Curly Bill Brocius. Some writers believe that he was only trying to enhance his reputation as a gunfighter when he claimed to have killed Curly Bill, and others believe that he actually did the deed. Curly Bill's body was never recovered, and there is reason to believe that he was alive and well, living in El Paso, Texas, in 1890.

Some time later, the body of John Ringo, one of the men Wyatt is known to have suspected in Morgan's murder, was found in the Dragoon Mountains. It was at the time and is today believed by some that Wyatt Earp killed him and left the body to rot. Wyatt is reported to have denied it. Sheriff Behan found the cause of death in the case of John Ringo to be suicide, and that's where he left it.

After Morgan's murder, Virgil and James and their wives decided to leave Tombstone for good. Wyatt, Warren, Doc Holiday, and a few others accompanied them as far as Tucson, where they would board the train to California. While they were waiting in the depot for the train to leave, someone spotted Ike Clanton and another of the cowboy faction, Frank Stilwell, lurking in the shadows of the railroad terminal. Wyatt had suspected both of them of being involved in Virgil's wounding and Morgan's murder, and he started moving toward them; the shotgun, which he carried concealed under his coat, was now out in the open and ready.

When Clanton and Stillwell saw Wyatt approaching them, they ran across the tracks and into the brush. Wyatt chased Stilwell down and killed him with a shotgun blast to the chest. He would later claim that the shooting was an accident caused by Stilwell grabbing the barrel of the shotgun after he caught up to him. Few people believed that story, the body was virtually blown apart by more than one shotgun blast.

Wyatt and his friends didn't wait around to explain what happened to Tucson law enforcement authorities. They immediately fled the scene and returned to Tombstone that same night. Stilwell's body wasn't discovered by railroad employees until the following afternoon.

Sheriff Bob Paul, who had by that time succeeded Charles Shibell in Pima County, obtained a warrant of arrest charging Wyatt Earp with the murder of Frank Stilwell. The warrant was sent by telegram to Tombstone, and John Behan once again went looking for Wyatt Earp to arrest him, but he was too late. Wyatt and Doc Holiday realized that they had overstayed their welcome in Arizona. Wyatt fled to California and Doc to Colorado, neither would ever step foot in Arizona again.

Virgil and James and their wives continued on to California. Virgil eventually became town marshal in Colton, California, where he served well and honorably for many years despite his crippled left arm. When his brothers weren't around to help him, Virgil was a good policeman.

After his sudden departure from Arizona, Wyatt Earp continued to drift through life, gambling, promoting himself and his schemes, and living by his wits until he was an old man. Josephine Marcus followed him to California, and they eventually married and remained together until Wyatt died in 1929. He was never particularly successful at anything, and during the years immediately before his death he and Josey lived on the charity of her family.

A motion picture entitled *The Passing of the Oklahoma Outlaws* was released in 1916. The six-reel silent movie was the only film ever made by *The Eagle Film Company*, which was the creation of three well-known and highly respected Oklahoma lawmen, Bill Tilghman, Ed Nix, and Chris Madsen. It told of their exploits dealing with notorious outlaws of their era. They probably stretched the truth a bit, but most of it was reasonably accurate, and the film played in many parts of the country to standing-room-only crowds for almost ten years. Bill Tilghman went on the lecture circuit for a time narrating the film and thrilling audiences with his personal accounts of derring-do. The three former lawmen became famous, and along with the fame came a lot of money.

Wyatt Earp undoubtedly heard about the movie – he may have even seen it – and he decided that it was time to cash-in on his own story. After several false starts on his own, he convinced a friend, John Flood, to collaborate with him and write the manuscript. As Wyatt told stories to him verbally, John Flood wrote. We can expect, of course, that Wyatt's version of the tales would be that most favorable to him.

When John Flood finished the manuscript, Wyatt tried to sell it to movie producers in Hollywood. He had always been a glib and persuasive talker when he wanted to be, and while making the rounds of the movie studios, he managed to meet and become friends with William S. Hart, Tom Mix, and other notables in the movie colony. They believed Wyatt's stories were true, and they listened to his yarns by the hour. Hart was especially smitten with Wyatt Earp; he once remarked to friends, "He *was* what I attempt to be in films." He remained devoted to Wyatt, and he was a pallbearer at Wyatt's funeral.

Even with the help of his new friends, Wyatt wasn't able to interest anyone in his manuscript. John Flood was an educated man, a mining engineer, but this was his first attempt at writing biography, and his manuscript simply wasn't coherent. A number of motion picture producers showed an interest in the story, but it needed to be told in a more professional manner.

Exactly how Stuart Lake got involved with Wyatt Earp isn't clear, but their mutual friend, Bat Masterson, may have had something to do with it.

Bat Masterson was one of the few of Wyatt's Dodge City associates to become a legitimate lawman. Following a short period of employment on the Dodge City Peace Commission, Bat Masterson was elected county sheriff. A few years later, he moved to Colorado and served as a deputy sheriff and town marshal in Trinidad and Creed for a few years. Then he became restless, tired of law enforcement and living conditions in the semi-rural West. He returned to the East, where he became a successful newspaper writer. He was primarily a sports reporter, but in between assignments he wrote a number of stories based on his personal experiences as a lawman in the West. To his credit, most of them are said to be reasonably factual.

Stuart Lake had been a reporter for *The New York Morning Telegram*, the newspaper for which Bat Masterson worked for a number of years as an editor and sports writer. He had since moved to Hollywood to try his hand at screen writing, but he was having difficulty breaking into the field. Bat Masterson may have suggested to Lake that he get in touch with Wyatt Earp, who he probably knew had friends and contacts in the motion picture industry. It may not have happened exactly that way, but in any event, Stuart Lake began collaborating with Wyatt Earp to write Earp's biography sometime in 1928.

In 1931 Stuart Lake published *Wyatt Earp, Frontier Marshal, a true account of Wyatt Earp's life as a frontier lawman as told to the author by the aging marshal himself.*

In reality, Stuart Lake and Wyatt Earp only had one relatively short face to face meeting, and the book is a heavily fictionalized mixture of Flood's manuscript and incidents liberally borrowed from Bat Masterson's stories published in New York newspapers and magazines. Wyatt, who died in 1929, never saw the manuscript.

That was the beginning of the *legend of Wyatt Earp*. In the years since it was first published, *Wyatt Earp, Frontier Marshal* has been the foundation of hundreds of other books, stories, and motion picture scripts. Some people today still believe that every word is the gospel truth, but it's not.

Stuart Lake admitted in a letter to a publisher in 1946 that Wyatt Earp never dictated a word to him. He admitted that *Wyatt Earp, Frontier Marshal* is romantic fiction, and all of the quotations attributed to Wyatt Earp in the book are his own. In other words, *it isn't necessarily the truth.*

Stuart Lake went on to become somewhat of a legend in his own right; he became a hugely successful screen writer with hits like *The Westerner*, *My Darling Clementine*, *Winchester '73,* and many others to his credit. He was a writer of *western fiction*, and he was very good at it. However, even his most ardent supporters admit that he often didn't get the history right. He was a true believer of John Ford's philosophy: *I don't portray the Frontier West as it was; I portray it as it should have been.*

John Behan served out the remainder of his term as Cochise County Sheriff, and by most reliable accounts, he did a commendable job, given the circumstances of the time and place.

Perhaps, Sheriff Behan did his job too well in some respects. County sheriffs collected taxes in Arizona in the early days, and the sheriff got to keep a percentage of the taxes collected as his pay. Many ranchers in the county had become accustomed to evading a good portion of their taxes; they were a long way from Tucson and they had rarely seen the Pima County Sheriff or one of his deputies. When they suddenly found themselves in the new Cochise County and Sheriff Behan came knocking on their doors demanding payment in full, they were unhappy to say the very least. When the next election came around, John Behan was defeated. It wasn't unusual for the times; until the law was changed relieving sheriffs of the duty to collect taxes, Arizona sheriffs who took their jobs seriously rarely got a second term in office.

Historians and writers have alleged in the years since that John Behan was friendly toward the cowboys and the rustlers because they were fellow Democrats, and that he turned a blind eye to their illegal cattle rustling across the Mexican border. The facts tell a different story.

Cattle rustling that moved animals both ways across the border was common for years before and after the turn of the century. Lots of people, Mexicans as well as Americans, were doing it from one end of the Mexican border to the other, in Texas as well as in New Mexico and Arizona. A county sheriff with a handful of deputies on horseback wasn't going to be able to stop it. John Behan as well as everyone else in the vicinity knew that to be a fact. So John decided to approach the problem from another angle; he ignored cattle brands and taxed the ranchers for every head of cattle that he found on their property. He and his chief deputy, Billy Breckenridge, laughed privately about the irony of taxing the ranchers for cattle that they had stolen. It didn't slow down the rustling to any great extent, but it raised a lot of money for the county treasury. And it may have cost the sheriff his job at election time.

John Clum and some of his cronies brought charges against John Behan after he left office for illegally collecting taxes, but the complaint came to nothing. It was summarily dismissed when John proved to the satisfaction of the court that he was legally entitled to collect the money and that he had accounted for every penny collected. Most everyone recognized the charges as politically motivated harassment; John Clum hadn't forgotten or forgiven.

John Behan needed a job, and he was offered a position as assistant superintendent of the territorial prison in Yuma. It was not so prestigious or financially rewarding a position as county sheriff, but it was a decent job with a salary that he could live on. He sold his house in Tombstone and all of his business interests in Cochise County, and he and Albert moved to Yuma.

He must have done a respectable job as assistant superintendent of the prison; although, there is reason to believe that he didn't particularly like the job. When the superintendent resigned on April 12, 1888, John Behan was appointed to replace him. He served as superintendent until April 7, 1890, when another political appointee replaced him in the patronage position. A new Republican territorial governor had been installed, and he too had political debts to pay.

John's tracks are difficult to follow after he left the prison job. He worked for a while as a clerk for the territorial legislature and then at several short-term jobs in the private sector. Then on June 3, 1893, he was sworn in as a U. S. Customs Inspector in El Paso, Texas, at a salary of four dollars a day.

There were few laws restricting the admission of aliens into the United States in those days. The Bureau of Immigration consisted of a Superintendent of Immigration and a couple of clerks who worked in an office in Washington, and there were no *inspectors* or enforcement officers of any stripe. U.S. Customs officers were assigned the additional duty to enforce the few immigration laws.

The Chinese Exclusion law was enacted in 1882, and it virtually barred the admission of ethnic Chinese aliens into the United States. At first Congress didn't provide for any additional immigration law enforcement measures; however, by 1893 it became apparent that the smuggling of Chinese aliens into the country was more widespread and involved more people than anyone had ever anticipated. It was estimated that fully one-third of the legally resident Chinese in El Paso, Texas, were involved in smuggling other Chinese into the country, and in New Mexico and

Arizona virtually all of the legally resident Chinese were involved.

A new position was created in the Bureau of Customs to deal with smugglers of Chinese aliens and to remove Chinese aliens who had managed to get into the country illegally. On March 12, 1894, John Behan was promoted to *Chinese Exclusion Agent* in the Bureau of Customs. His salary was set at six dollars a day, not much by today's standards, but a substantial raise in pay for the times. I can't confirm that he was the *first* such officer appointed, but he was certainly among the first.

Police and county sheriffs along the border occasionally encountered illegal Chinese aliens, but then they didn’t know what to do with them. John Behan and his fellow Chinese Exclusion Agents traveled through the border states collecting the illegal aliens and presenting them to a court for orders of deportation. Under the provisions of the Chinese Exclusion Act, any justice of the peace, judge, or commissioner could order a Chinese alien deported. With deportation order in hand, the federal officer would take the Chinese person to the nearest port of entry on the border and deport him. They apparently encountered no particular problems with deporting Chinese aliens into Mexico at that time. We can only guess at the number of Chinese who may have entered the United States at seaports on the West Coast and then found themselves suddenly deported to Mexico.

John Behan’s official station was El Paso, Texas, but he seems to have spent most of his time traveling in New Mexico and Arizona by train, wagon, and horseback. His diary listing his travels, his expenses, and his *inspections* is in possession of the

Arizona Historical Society museum in Tucson. It's obvious that the man traveled constantly, and he rarely got home to El Paso.

Today's Border Patrol agents who complain about being detailed away from home should read this man's diary. Of course, there were advantages to traveling on government business in those days; he got two dollars a day subsistence in addition to his salary.

Apparently, by the summer of 1897, John had had enough of the constant traveling in pursuit of Chinese aliens. He was offered a position as a finance officer at Fort Bliss, and he returned to the United States Army. He served in the Quartermaster Corps in Cuba during the Spanish American War. After the war, he returned to the Bureau of Customs and was appointed Deputy Collector of Customs at Yuma, Arizona. He left that position in 1900 to return to the U.S. Army once again, and he served in China during the Boxer Rebellion. (It isn't clear whether he was a commissioned officer or a civilian employee of the army at that time; the official army records were destroyed in a fire. It makes little difference to our story, anyway.)

John Behan left the army for the last time in 1901 when he returned from China. He then became part-owner and business manager of the *Tucson Citizen*, one of the territory's early newspapers. It was a unstable arrangement almost from the beginning, and after a protracted disagreement with his partner over editorial policy and business practices, they dissolved the partnership and John resigned.

John next worked as purchasing agent for a construction company in El Paso, Texas. Then in 1906, he decided to throw his hat into the political ring again, and he ran for Sheriff of El Paso County. Although he had ringing endorsements from several Arizona newspapers referring to him as "modest as a woman, honest as Paul, and brave as Caesar" and "well and favorably known throughout this territory," he lost the election.

Following his defeat at the polls, he was offered a job with Southern Pacific Railroad to be in charge of the commissary department during the construction of the railroad's branch line, the *Ferrocarril Sur-Pacifico de Mexico,* from Nogales, Arizona, to Guaymas, Sonora. The word *commissary* is a little misleading here; he was responsible for purchasing, transportation, and storage of virtually all of the materials, equipment, and supplies for this major construction project. He continued in that position until his failing health forced him to resign in 1911.

John Behan then returned to Tucson, Arizona, to live out the rest of his life in retirement. He died of complications of Bright's disease in 1912. His grave in Tucson's Holy Hope Cemetery is rarely visited today, his rightful place in Arizona history having been stolen from him by all of the promoters, pseudo *historians*, and fiction writers hyping the image of Wyatt Earp over the years. And that's a shame!

In January of 1881, in the town of Charleston, eleven miles southwest of Tombstone, a gambler and drifter named Michael O'Rourke, who was better known as *Johnny-Behind-The-Deuce*, shot and killed a mining engineer. He was arrested by the Charleston town marshal and taken to jail in Tombstone. A short time later, a group of miners tried to take him out of the jail and lynch him. Historians, fiction writers, and moviemakers, one after the other, over and over, have told of how Marshal Wyatt Earp saved the man's life: *Alone and unafraid, Marshal Earp held the crowd at bay with cold nerves, steely eyes, and a ten-gauge shotgun.* It didn't happen that way!

According to John Clum's *Tombstone Epitaph* published at the time it occurred: "The unruly mob was turned away by Pima County Deputy Sheriff John Behan, Town Marshal Ben Sippy, and Deputy U.S. Marshal Virgil Earp." If Wyatt Earp had been anywhere in the neighborhood that night, you can be sure that John Clum would not have missed the opportunity to include him in the action. He wasn't there!

On another occasion, Wyatt and Virgil Earp were playing cards with Doc Holiday at the Oriental Saloon, when Doc and Milton Joyce, the owner of the saloon, got into a heated argument. Doc was drunk, as usual, and Joyce had been drinking, too. When Doc insulted him, Joyce got a shotgun from behind the bar, and in a rather loud voice he threatened to shoot Holiday and the Earps, too. John Behan happened to be walking by on the sidewalk outside, and he heard the threats. Through a window he could see Joyce holding the shotgun on Holiday and the Earps. He entered the saloon by a side entrance, quietly crept up behind Joyce, pinned the man's arms to his sides, and took the shotgun away from him. As he marched Milton Joyce off to jail, he commented, "There's been enough killing around here." The Earps and Holiday began to breathe again. That incident really happened; so why don't we ever see that scene in the movies?

While he was assistant superintendent of the territorial prison, John Behan was credited with single-handedly closing the main gate in the face of rioting prisoners and preventing a prison break. That incident was reported in the Yuma newspaper at the time, and John Behan was commended for his bravery in the face of extreme danger, but that incident is never mentioned in any of the dozens of books and movies.

During his lifetime, no one other than a few disgruntled political opponents ever questioned John Behan's competence, his integrity, or his courage; although, a few folks did question his morals and his judgment when it came to the fairer sex. To his credit, he seems to have kept his affairs private, which is more than can be said for many politicians of his time…or of any time since.

In recognition of John Harrris Behan's patriotism, valor, fidelity, and ability and the esteem in which he was held by his peers and Arizona law enforcement officers, Secretary of the Territory George U. Young, acting on behalf of Governor Richard Elihu Sloan, issued a proclamation on December 14, 1910 appointing him a railroad policeman with the powers of peace officer throughout the territory. It was a ceremonial honor to be sure; he was then sixty-five years old and his law enforcement days were behind him, but it was nevertheless a significant honor.

John Behan was a respected father, successful businessman, lawman, soldier, and public servant for many years. He was a true pioneer in every sense of the word, and he made a positive contribution to the development of early Arizona. Had he been born a hundred years later, he would have worn *our green*, no doubt about it.

Josephine (Marcus) Earp and Albert Behan remained close for many years. They corresponded regularly, and Albert seems to have looked upon her as he would an older sister. She visited with John and Albert on at least one occasion when they were living in Yuma and John was superintendent of the prison. I don't know if Wyatt Earp accompanied her on that trip, but I believe it's unlikely that he did. The arrest warrant for the murder of Frank Stilwell was still outstanding in Arizona, and Wyatt Earp had good reason not to cross the river.

Albert Behan became a mounted customs inspector in 1913. He was stationed in El Paso, Texas, where he patrolled the border on horseback and by automobile enforcing the United States customs laws until 1928.

I intended this story to be about John Behan, not about Wyatt Earp, Tombstone, or the infamous gunfight at the O.K. Corral. I was going to end it here, but then I got a letter in the mail:

Dear Gene:

Words cannot express my gratitude for your undertaking on my behalf to set the record straight on my character and career. The Good Lord knows how I have suffered at the hands of those who, over the years, have attempted to confer some kind of Old West sainthood upon Wyatt Earp. I am especially heartened by your detailed description of my myriad accomplishments after my term as

Sheriff of Cochise County. Few know of them.

Reputations, though, are not zero sum faro games. It is not necessary to go after Wyatt to save me. Such an assault, even armed with the truth, may prove counterproductive. Folks will make it ALL ABOUT WYATT again, and there's been quite enough of that! Besides, I hold no ill will towards Wyatt. Virgil was more to my liking, but Wyatt and Morg were tolerable sorts.

Gals like Josie come and go; the West was full of them, and I held no grudge against Wyatt over Josie.

I strived mightily to keep the Earps as friends. I even asked Wyatt to partner up with me at first. But once he went after the local ranchers, first with that Army mule business, then with the horse stealing affair, I had to keep my distance, at least publicly. He should have come to me first. But that's Wyatt! He was never one to stop and think before he jumped.

Once again, thank you for the kindnesses and respect I have rarely been shown.

With warmest regards,

John Harris Behan

Americans take their legends seriously. I didn't

realize how seriously until I took a shot at Wyatt Earp. John Behan makes a good point when he says that this will be *all about Wyatt* again, if I'm not careful. I don't want that. I just want folks to know that the *pseudo* historians and western fiction writers are wrong when they denigrate the memory of John Behan. He wasn't a coward or a crook. He was a good man trying to do his best in a difficult time, and he did well.

Sorry, Wyatt, that I had to step on your toes to get my point across.

\+ + + + + + +

Note: My thanks to David Barrow Churchill, lawyer, amateur historian, fellow scribbler, and friend, for his help in bringing this story back into perspective and straightening me out on a few points that I had missed in my research. David wrote the letter from John Behan reminding me that it isn't necessary to destroy the memory of one man in order to honor another. He also reminded me that two people honestly and objectively considering the same set of facts can arrive at different conclusions. - GB

The Patroit

by

Ed Woods

I came awake the other night
Was late November and dark
Faint sound I heard was strange
To these old ringing ears
Tramping of many ruffled feet
In the snow and the mud

A voice was sayin' to the beat
Rally 'round the flag boys
They are stealin' the Constitution
And bring yer muskets, too

The drum roll was long
Kept tapping to the shout
In time with the notes
Played upon that little fife
Was music to my ears
Seemed to rouse my ragged fears

Again that voice from the past

Recuerdos

Raised up that rousing cry
Rally 'round the flag boys
The aliens, felons, and politicians
Are stealin' this land we tilth
A spreadin' lies, untruths, and filth
They are tearin' up the sacred paper
On which the citizens rely
Lived honestly, coveted for so long
Served our purpose, they tear it down

So up all you citizens and brothers
Remember the blood that it cost
Forget not our brothers in arms
Your citizenship they are stealing
In the cold of the night
Rally 'round the flag boys
Resist with all your might
And bring yer muskets, too

There before my eyes a little fellow
With cloth bound cold feet
Playin' that tune on a little fife
The drummer marched next to him
There next old Glory held high
The fourth shouldered his musket

The vision fades from my view
And I set up in my bed
Recognized old George, Ben, and dad
So I pulled on my clothes and boots
And I started out the door
The wife said hurry back
And don't forget your gun

Recuerdos

They are stealin' our great land
Trampling upon the truth
Bring your vigilance and gun at hand
Rally 'round those long forgotten men
As they pass to guard freedoms land
My cry joins theirs as we march
Arise you citizens, protect your land

Rally 'round this battered banner
Protect your freedom and this land
Guard citizenship with all your might
It's the last in this world, you see
Rid us of felons, aliens, and bad
politicians
Walk with pride and dignity
And don't forget your muskets, boys

December 2000

\+ + + + + + +

The Authors,

in the order in which their work first appears.

Edward G. (Ed) Woods, who wrote the poems ***I am a Citizen*** and ***The Patriot*** *and* the stories ***Those Were The Days!*** and ***Border Patrol Airline***, entered the Border Patrol as a Patrol Inspector (trainee) in September of 1957 at Chula Vista, California, in the 71st session of the Border Patrol Academy. After having learned to fly on the GI Bill, he was promoted to Border Patrol Pilot in January of 1961. He retired from the Border Patrol as a sector pilot in Livermore, California, in March of 1978.

Ed and his wife, Betty, presently live in Weiser, Idaho, where he builds and flies his own airplanes. He is known as the *Grumpy ol' Geezer from Weiser.*

Eugene M. (Gene) Botts, who collected and edited these stories and wrote ***Jeff Milton***, ***We Must Have Done Something Right!***, and ***A Man Much Maligned*** entered the Border Patrol at Calexico, California, on October 14, 1957, as a Patrol Inspector (trainee) in the 71st session of the Border Patrol Academy. He served in the Border Patrol in California and Minnesota until 1964, when he transferred to Chicago as an Immigrant Inspector. In 1966, he transferred to Investigations where he spent the balance of his career, retiring in January of 1985 as Assistant District Director for Investigations in New Orleans, Louisiana. He presently resides in Fernandina Beach, Florida.

Orville C. Lewis, who wrote ***Big Game Hunting*** and ***Was It That Long Ago?***, entered the Border Patrol at El Paso, Texas, on August 8, 1955, as a Patrol Inspector (trainee) in the 62nd session of the Border Patrol Academy. In September of 1957, he was detailed from the El Paso station to the academy as a firearms and physical training instructor. What was intended to be a six weeks detail lasted until November of 1961. In September of 1962, he was transferred to Livermore, California, where he served as Special Detail Officer, Intelligence Officer, and ultimately Assistant Chief Patrol Inspector. He retired on December 29, 1979, and he continues to reside in Livermore with his wife Billie.

Walter V. Edwards, who wrote ***The Best Job We Ever*** Had, entered the Border Patrol as a Patrol Inspector (trainee) on May 10, 1951, at El Paso, Texas. He subsequently served in the Border Patrol until August of 1964, rising to the level of Assistant Chief Patrol Inspector. He then transferred to the Dallas, Texas, office of the INS where he served as a Criminal Investigator, Assistant Officer-in-Charge, and then Officer-in-Charge until September of 1973, when he was appointed District Director at Denver, Colorado. On January 19, 1976, he was appointed Associate Regional Commissioner for Enforcement in Dallas, Texas, the position from which he retired on March 23,

1979. Since retirement, he has been very active in the Fraternal Order of Retired Border Patrol Officers and an active supporter of the Border Patrol Museum. He currently serves on the Board of Trustees of the Border Patrol Museum and Memorial Library Foundation. He and his wife Annetta live in Plano, Texas.

Gerald A. (Jerry) Dahlberg, who wrote ***Arizona Justice*** and ***A Dog's Life***, entered the Border Patrol as a Patrol Inspector (trainee) in May of 1950 in the 39th session of the Border Patrol Academy. Thereafter, he served five years in the Border Patrol in Texas and California, six years as an Immigrant Inspector in various locations, and the balance of his career as an Investigator. He currently resides in Ione, California, with his wife, Lorraine.

Robert D. (Bob) McCord, who wrote ***Snakes Alive***, entered the Border Patrol at Brownsville, Texas, on May 6th 1957 as a Patrol Inspector (trainee). After completing probation, he was transferred to Kingsville, Texas. In 1960, he transferred to Florida, serving in Melbourne and Miami until 1962 when he was transferred to Harlingen, Texas. In 1966, he was promoted to Criminal Investigator in San Francisco, California, where he served for the next eight years. In 1978, he returned to the Border Patrol as Assistant Chief Patrol Agent in Chula Vista, California, where he served until he was appointed Assistant Regional Commissioner, Border Patrol in the Southern Region (Dallas, Texas). In 1980 he was promoted to Chief Patrol Agent in Yuma, Arizona, where he remained until his retirement on December 31, 1983.

Since his retirement Bob has been active in the Fraternal Order of Retired Border Patrol Officers, serving one term as Chairman of the Board of Directors and one term as President. He and Barbara, his wife of more than fifty years, now live in Kingman, Arizona. They have three grown children and five grandchildren.

William R. (Bill) Botts, who wrote ***Standoff at the Salton Sea,*** entered the Border Patrol as a Patrol Agent (trainee) at El Centro, California on April 8, 1985, in the 177th session of the Border Patrol Academy. He was promoted to Senior Patrol Agent in July of 1988 and to Supervisory Patrol Agent in September of 1992. In June of 1998, he was promoted to Assistant Patrol Agent-in-Charge at Nogales, Arizona, and in November of 2001, he became Patrol Agent-in-Charge at Gulfport, Mississippi, where he is currently serving.

Brenda Tisdale, who wrote ***Gerry Tisdale, the scouts and the dogs***, was the wife of Assistant Chief Patrol Agent Gerry Tisdale for more than thirty years. Although Brenda was never a Patrol Agent, she is certainly a member of the Border Patrol family and uniquely qualified to add to this collection of Border Patrol stories.

Brenda was the very capable manager of the Gift Shop at the Border Patrol Museum in El Paso, Texas, from 1996 until 2001, when she was appointed curator of the museum. Her dedication to the Border Patrol and to the cause of our museum is well-known by Border Patrol officers, past and present.

Robert J. (Bob) Carney, who wrote ***War Surplus*** first entered the Border Patrol as a Patrol Agent (trainee) on September 21, 1988, in the 226 class at the Border Patrol Academy. He was stationed at Imperial Beach, California. In April of 1996, he was promoted to Senior Patrol Agent, and in September of 1997, he was promoted to Supervisory Patrol Agent. In August of 2004, he was transferred to Air Operations at El Centro, California, where he currently serves as an Aircraft Pilot. He is married to Refugio (Cuca) Carney, a Supervisory Patrol Agent at the Brownfield station in the San Diego Sector. Mr. Carney also continues to serve as a Lieutenant Colonel in the United States Army Reserve.

Roger P. (Buck) Brandemuehl, who wrote ***A Very Mobile Organization*** and ***Galveston, Oh Galveston***, entered the Border Patrol as a Patrol Inspector (trainee) on August 1, 1956, at Yuma, Arizona. During his thirty year career with the INS, he served as Patrol Inspector, an Immigrant Inspector, a Deportation Officer, a Criminal Investigator, Assistant Officer-in-Charge of a sub-office, Assistant District Director for Investigations, Supervisory Patrol Agent, Intelligence Officer, Deputy Chief Patrol Agent, and Chief Patrol Agent. He was the Assistant Commissioner for Border Patrol (Chief of the Border Patrol) when he retired from the INS in July of 1986.

After retiring from the INS, Buck assumed the position of President of Eagle Security Enterprises, a private security company. He has also been active in the Fraternal Order of Retired Border Patrol Officers, and he is currently a member of the Board of Trustees of the National Border Patrol Museum and Memorial Library

Foundation. He resides in Temple, Texas, with his wife, Ada, where he is an active member of the Temple Bible Church. The Brandemuehls have three grown children, Pam Ela, Michael, and Christi.

William J. (Bill) Chambers, who wrote ***You Have the Right to Remain Silent***, entered the Border Patrol on October 10, 1950, at Harlingen, Texas, as a security officer. He was promoted to Patrol Inspector on April 17, 1951, transferred to El Paso, Texas, and attended the 44th session of the Border Patrol Academy in Las Cruces, New Mexico. After finishing training, he was transferred back to Harlingen, Texas, to work as a Patrol Inspector. On August 1, 1955, he became the director of the Alien Processing Center in Eagle Pass, Texas. On April 8, 1963, he transferred to Del Rio, Texas, where he served as Officer-in-Charge of the Port of Entry until June 10, 1973, when he was transferred to Houston, Texas, where he served first as Officer-in-Charge and later as Assistant District Director. On April 24, 1977, he was promoted to District Director at Dallas, Texas, where he served until retirement on December 2, 1983. Since his retirement, Bill has been active in the Fraternal Order of Retired Border Patrol Officers, serving two terms on the board of directors, one of which was as chairman of the board. He and his wife, Margie, currently reside in Richardson, Texas.

Dale A. Musegades, who wrote ***The Cripple Was Crooked***, entered the Border Patrol as a Patrol Inspector (trainee) at Calexico, California on February 20, 1961, in the 77th session of the Border Patrol Academy. Thirty-two years later, after serving continuously in the Border Patrol at stations in California, Arizona, and Texas, he retired as Chief Patrol Agent in El Paso, Texas. He presently resides in Tucson, Arizona.

Robert J. (Bob) Stille, who wrote ***Giant Jean Ferre*** and ***The Salt and Pepper Tag Team***, entered the Border Patrol on September 25, 1958, in the 72nd session of the Border Patrol Academy. In August of 1971, he was promoted to Supervisory Patrol Inspector in Newport, Vermont. Thereafter, he served as Patrol Agent in Charge at Indio, Calexico, and Campo, California, before retiring on September 30, 1990. He presently resides in New Mexico with his wife, Yvonne.

Owen W. (Wes) Selman, who wrote the poem ***Memories of Sign-Cutting*** and the short story ***Involuntary Transfer to Customs***, entered the Border Patrol as a Patrol Inspector (trainee) in May of 1956 at Chula Vista, California. He was a member of the 65th session of the Border Patrol Academy. In February of 1962, he left the Border Patrol to become an Immigrant Inspector serving at Cleveland, Ohio, Eagle Pass, Texas, and Douglas, Arizona. He retired from the INS on January 3, 1984 as a Supervisory Immigrant Inspector. He presently resides in Silver City, New Mexico.

Ray Harris, who wrote ***The Nasty Boys***, entered the Border Patrol on September 15, 1980 as a Patrol Agent (trainee), after serving thirteen years in the United States Marine Corps as an aircraft electronics technician in Japan, Viet Nam, and other *fun* places. As he says, he exchanged one green uniform for another with only about two weeks break in between. He served in the Border Patrol at Presidio, Texas, Nogales, Arizona, and New Orleans, Louisiana, before being promoted to Supervisory Patrol Agent in Riverside, California. He later became a Special Agent in the INS office in San Bernardino, California, from which position he retired on May 1, 2002. He currently resides in La Habra, California.

Mr. Harris's overabundance of energy keeps him more active than most in retirement. He has worked as a veteran's representative for Riverside County, California, as a personnel background investigator for a casino in Indio, California, and two tours as a civilian contractor training military border guards in Pakistan. He is also a writer, currently working on a novel set in the Border Patrol, which should be a thriller.

For many years on his own time and at his own expense, Mr. Harris has maintained an unofficial U.S. Border Patrol website (http://www.honorfirst.com) on the Internet, which presents Border Patrol officers, their training, and their duties in a most favorable light. His efforts have resulted in hundreds of young men and women choosing the Border Patrol as a career.

Arno A. (Hank) Henderson, who wrote ***A Guy Could Get Hurt In This Job***, entered the Border Patrol as a Patrol Inspector (trainee) at McAllen, Texas, on January 10, 1949. In January of 1962, he was promoted the Supervisory Patrol Inspector at Warroad, Minnesota, from which position he retired in May of

1974. He continues to reside in Warroad with his wife, Virginia. In retirement he has been active farming, Mink and cattle ranching, and in sailing, boating and fishing on Lake of the Woods. He is also the author of the autobiography *No Flag For My Coffin*, which is on sale at the Border Patrol Museum gift shop.

Alvin Braunstein, who wrote ***Goodbye Mama***, entered the Border Patrol at Del Rio, Texas, as a Patrol Inspector (trainee) in August of 1957, in the 70th session of the Border Patrol Academy. In 1962, he was promoted to Immigrant Inspector in Chicago. He later served as Assistant Officer in Charge at Eagle Pass, Texas, Supervisory Immigrant Inspector in Los Angeles, and in staff positions at the Southwest Regional Office and the Central Office in Washington, D.C. He retired in 1981, and he presently resides in San Antonio, Texas.

W.O. (Dub) Covington, who wrote ***Detail to Langtry***, entered the Border Patrol as a Patrol Inspector (trainee) in the fall of 1957 in the 71st session of the Border Patrol Academy. He later became a Border Patrol pilot and served in that position in Texas for more than twenty years. Shortly after submitting ***Detail to Langtry***, Mr. Covington passed away on December 19, 2003, at the age of seventy-seven. He is missed.

John Evangelist, who wrote the autobiography from which ***John Evangelist, A Border Patrol Pilot*** was taken, entered the Border Patrol on June 27, 1955, in the 61st session of the Border Patrol Academy. He retired on December 31, 1977, and he passed away in El Centro, California, on August 18, 2002. He describes his career in the Border Patrol in detail in his story.

Timothy N. (Tim) Waller, who wrote ***Keep Out!***, entered the Border Patrol as a Patrol Inspector (trainee) on April 16, 1961, at El Paso, Texas, in the 80th session of the Border Patrol Academy. In 1964, he was transferred to Hebronville, Texas, and in 1971, he was promoted to Senior Patrol Inspector at Eagle Pass, Texas. In 1975, he transferred to Investigations at Salt Lake City, Utah, from which position he retired on November 30, 1993. He and his wife, Vicky, continue to reside in Salt Lake City.

In retirement, Tim maintains a rather large email list of INS retirees and others, and he keeps us informed of current happenings among the members of the old INS extended family.

Norman M. Howe, who wrote ***The Suggestion Box***, entered the Border Patrol as a Patrol Inspector (trainee) at Las Cruces, New Mexico, on October 10, 1957, in the 71st session of the Border Patrol Academy. He retired from the Immigration and Naturalization Service as an Immigration Examiner at San Antonio, Texas, on November 1, 1987. He presently resides with his wife, Beverly, in Lakehills, Texas.

\+ \+ \+ \+ \+ \+ \+